JUSTICE
FOR
COLETTE

JUSTICE
FOR
COLETTE

My daughter was murdered – I never gave up
hope of her killer being found. He was finally
caught after 26 years ...

JACQUI KIRKBY
WITH VERONICA CLARK

JOHN BLAKE

Published by John Blake Publishing Ltd,
3 Bramber Court, 2 Bramber Road,
London W14 9PB, England

www.johnblakepublishing.co.uk

www.facebook.com/Johnblakepub   facebook

twitter.com/johnblakepub   twitter

First published in paperback in 2012

ISBN: 9781843587613

British Library Cataloguing-in-Publication Data:

A catalogue record for this book is available from the British Library.

Design by www.envydesign.co.uk

Printed and bound by CPI Group (UK) Ltd,
Croydon, CR0 4YY

3 5 7 9 10 8 6 4 2

Papers used by John Blake Publishing are natural,
recyclable products made from wood grown in sustainable forests.
The manufacturing processes conform to the environmental
regulations of the country of origin.

Every attempt has been made to contact the relevant copyright-
holders, but some were unobtainable. We would be grateful if the
appropriate people could contact us.

To Colette, our lovely, happy and caring girl.
Rest in peace our angel. No one can
harm you now.

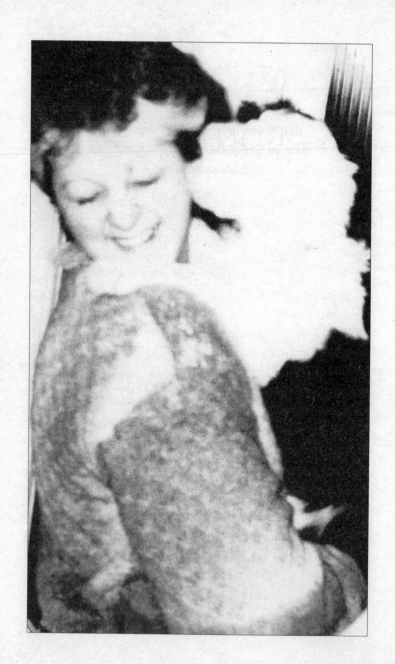

CONTENTS

ACKNOWLEDGEMENTS

There are many people I'd like to thank for their support over the years. Firstly, I'd like to say a huge thank you to all my family, particularly my son Mark and my mother Joyce. Also my gratitude goes to my brother Michael and sister-in-law Sue, and to all the family and friends who have helped and encouraged me over the years. Special thanks to those who had hoped to see justice be done but sadly passed away before this could happen.

My humble gratitude goes to my dear friend Sue Copley, who sat endlessly by my bed during those horrific early days and who has continued to support me throughout the rest of my life. Also my very dear friends Ann Carnegie Brown, Kay Woodhall and Val Woodford, who helped me keep my sanity in the early days of the murder inquiry.

To all the officers from Nottinghamshire police who worked tirelessly around the clock to catch Colette's killer. But, most of all, my heartfelt thanks goes to now retired Detective Superintendent Kevin Flint for his compassion, patience and determination that one day the man responsible for taking my beautiful daughter's life would be jailed. Kevin promised me that we would get our day in court and, thanks to him and his fantastic team, we did. There are not enough words to express my gratitude to you. You are a gentleman and I thank you sincerely from the bottom of my heart.

Kevin received the Queen's Medal for Distinguished Service, presented to him by Prince Charles at Buckingham Palace. It marked a fitting end to his 34 years' service in the police force. Many people can sleep safer at night thanks to Kevin and his team.

Thank you also to all the forensic scientists who worked on Colette's case over the many years that followed, particularly the brilliant Tim Clayton.

Finally to my very dear friend and ghostwriter Veronica Clark, for the empathy and respect that she has shown throughout the process of writing this book. Without her, none of this would have been possible. Not only have we written this book together, but I have also gained in her a lifelong friend.

INTRODUCTION

It is often said that, without hope, you have nothing. I have written this book to give hope to those who find themselves in the same dreadful position that we did. I am talking about the families who have lost a loved one in the most callous and brutal way imaginable – murder.

We've all seen them – the grieving families on the TV, staring out from the court steps, weeping towards the cameras. They are captured forever on film as they try to come to terms with their deep loss. For onlookers it is sad, but not forever. Long after the cameras and journalists have packed up and gone away, those families must live with that grief for the rest of their lives.

Murder leaves a huge void in your heart and soul that can never be filled. The pain doesn't get any easier; you just learn to live with it. Most families in this situation get their conclusion a year or so after an arrest is made. Most of the time and, in the case of murder, an arrest usually follows pretty quickly; in our case, it didn't. We had to wait more than a quarter of a century for justice for my lovely daughter Colette. During that time, the grief not only destroyed us one by one, it also split up my family, cost me my marriage and at times threatened my sanity. You continue to mourn for your loved one, and being the one left behind is sometimes a very lonely place to be.

It was my intention to write this book to give hope to other families that have gone, or are going, through the hell that we have endured for 26 long years. I also want to tell people what really happens to the other victims – those left behind – in these situations. Murder doesn't stop at the crime itself. By its very nature, it sends shockwaves through entire families, destroying everything in its path. This ripple effect hurts every single person it touches, most of all the immediate family. They will try, as we did, to piece their fragmented lives back together, but it's almost impossible. Once those lives have been smashed to smithereens by the impact of murder, there is no turning back. Your life changes forever in an instant.

This book is about the impact of such a deep and sudden loss, and how I grieved for my beautiful daughter. But it is also a book of hope – how I always believed that the police would catch her killer. It is written in memory of my lovely daughter Colette. I hope that, by reading it, you will gain a valuable insight into what happens behind the doors of those grieving family homes up and down the country.

INTRODUCTION

Colette's murder was one of the biggest and longest manhunts that Britain has ever seen. At its peak the inquiry had over 50 detectives working on it, day and night. It was led by no less than four senior investigating officers with one common goal – to catch her killer.

It took 26 years, but the police finally got their man and I got my justice. This unique experience has taught me one thing – never to give up hope. At times, I felt like doing so, but I never did, for without hope you have nothing.

As I started to write this book, I thought of happy times and fond memories, but they were often overshadowed by bad ones. It was difficult to put pen to paper and recall happy memories but I knew that I must do so. When I see her smiling face, I don't see Colette Aram the murder victim, I see Colette Aram my beautiful little girl. She had a smile that could light up a room, a wicked sense of humour and an infectious laugh. She wasn't an angel, no one is, but she was deeply treasured – she was my lovely Colette.

I dedicate this book not only to Colette but also to my wonderful son Mark. Despite his own private torment, he has been a continuous support to me and his father Tony throughout those 26 years. We love you, Mark, and feel honoured to call you our son.

So, this book is for her. A tribute to Colette – a very special girl and loving daughter who we were blessed with and allowed to share 16 years of blissful life with. We all love and miss you, Colette, but this is for you, my love. This is our justice for Colette.

Here is my story.

CHAPTER 1

GROWING UP

It was 1961 – the beginning of the Swinging Sixties – and times were good. Elvis Presley was riding high in the charts and change was in the air. A teenage revolution was reverberating through society with clothes, attitudes and music to show it. It would be another two years before the Beatles broke into the charts, singing about love and pleading with screaming girls to let them hold their hands. Expectations were as high as the miniskirts of the women who wore them. It was a buoyant time to be young, free and single. And I was.

I had my whole life mapped out in front of me. I was training to become a hairdresser at a salon in Nottingham. Even though my mother had divorced, she'd scrimped and saved all of her money working as a dressmaker for a local designer to put me through an apprenticeship so that I could have the career of my dreams.

I was just 16 years old when my uncle Joe tried to set me up on a blind date with a boy he knew from work.

'His name's Anthony but we all call him Tony,' he began. 'He looks like Elvis, but he's not like him at all. Tony's a nice lad, very quiet.'

'I prefer Cliff Richard,' I said, winking at him, as I busied myself curling my mum Joyce's hair in the living room.

'You could do much worse, Jacqui,' Uncle Joe told me. 'He's not like all those boys who like to go out drinking and chasing girls. Tony's a good lad.'

I finally relented and allowed Uncle Joe to fix me up on a date with this mystery Elvis lookalike.

'What have I let myself in for?' I chuckled to Mum after my uncle had closed the door behind him.

I was still a baby really, but I'd never made a secret of the fact that I wanted to settle down young and start a family. I wasn't like other girls my age who wanted to explore the freedom and the sexual revolution of these new and exciting times. I couldn't wait to become a mother instead. I was desperate to grow up, get a place of my own and be a good mother – it was all I'd ever dreamed of since I was a little girl.

My father Arthur was the managing director of an engineering company in Nottingham. He had a well-paid job and we – Mum, Dad, me and my younger brother Michael – lived in a house owned by Dad's company. However, my dad had an affair with his secretary. Mum was heartbroken, and, to rub salt into the wound, he then decided that he no longer wanted us; he wanted a new life with Audrey, his new woman. Dad moved out of our beloved family home and set up home with Audrey, and it wasn't long before we were turfed out too.

Our family unit had been shattered and we had nowhere to live. We'd gone from a charmed life to brassy broke. In the end, Mum went to live with my grandmother, taking Michael, then aged just eight, with her. Meanwhile, I was dispatched to stay with my mother's youngest sister Mary. She and her husband Roy had just had their first child – a little girl called Susan – so I helped out with the baby and, as she grew, Susan and I became very close. She was the sister that I never had.

My parents' divorce happened when I was just 12 years old. Like most girls of that age, I was self-conscious and unsure of myself and, witnessing the mess of it all, I somehow thought I was to blame. Divorce was very unusual back in the Sixties, so I was different to all my friends – when I lost my family unit, it was as though I'd lost my way in life too. Children can take divorce very personally, and I did.

Growing up through this traumatic time made me crave the security of a loving family of my own. It became my dream, my goal. It doesn't sound very much, especially these days, to admit that all you want to be is a mother and housewife. But I didn't care about money or belongings. I just wanted to find the man of my dreams, get married and have children of my own to love. Now, four years after my parents' divorce, aged 16, I now had a blind date to contend with.

There was a knock at our front door. I opened it to

find a nervous Tony stood alongside Uncle Joe, who was leading proceedings.

'Jacqui, this is Tony,' he said, with a sweep of his upturned palm. 'Tony, this is Jacqui. There you have it – now you've both been formally introduced.'

I looked at Tony. It felt stilted and awkward standing there, and Uncle Joe sensed it.

'Right, is your mother in, Jacqui?' Uncle Joe enquired suddenly. 'I'm gasping for a cuppa.' With that, he pushed straight past me, leaving me on the doorstep with my blind date.

Tony was tall, dark and handsome and wearing a smart khaki suit that looked very expensive. His black, glossy hair was combed back into a trendy Elvis-style quiff. Still, he looked awkward. He looked down at his feet rather than making direct eye contact. Even so, I knew there and then that he was quite a catch and that I'd be daft to turn this opportunity down.

'I won't be a mo,' I said, grabbing my coat off the peg in the hallway before dashing out the front door to Tony's car outside the garden gate.

'Do you fancy a drink at a pub?' Tony asked as he started up the engine of his dark-green Morris Minor.

I nodded politely and soon we were on our way – I felt as if all my dreams had come true in that single moment.

Tony was 20 years old, and I thought he was the most sophisticated man that I'd ever met. I didn't drink back then, so, when he asked me what I wanted, I said an orange juice. I felt awkward, young and foolish – a schoolgirl in high heels and earrings. I was so desperate to impress this older, good-looking man that I tried hard to look relaxed and comfortable but I was far from it.

Thankfully, Tony was easy to talk to. We spoke about all kinds of things that afternoon – from my meddling uncle Joe to my work as a hairdresser. Tony explained about his work and told me that he was an only child. Soon the hours had flown past. By the end of the evening, I realised that, while he was shy, Tony was hardworking, fun and had a good sense of humour. In short, he made me laugh. The only sticking point came when I discovered that he didn't like dancing. It was my one big passion. I'd danced all my life and had even competed at shows for ballroom dancing. But, I reasoned, it was a small price to pay for the man of my dreams.

That evening, as he dropped me back home, Tony bent forward and gave me a peck on the cheek. I felt my face flush as he did so.

'I'd like to see you again, Jacqui, if that's all right?' he asked.

I nodded and we set another date for the end of the week.

That Saturday, I spent all afternoon getting ready. I made sure that I applied my make-up so it looked light and natural and I spent ages blow-drying and styling my hair. My mum had made me a Brigitte Bardot-style dress – it was all the rage at the time. The dress was white and lilac gingham and it had a neat little white bodice stitched on the front. I loved it and felt a million dollars every time I wore it. I slipped on a pair of white kitten-heel sandals and waited by the window, looking out for Tony's car.

Soon, I saw the little green Morris Minor slowly weave its way up our street and park outside my house.

When I opened the door to Tony, I noticed there were two older people sitting in his car – a man in the back and a woman in the front. The woman was staring right at me.

That must be his mother, I thought.

'Er, you don't mind if I drop my mum and dad off, do you?' said Tony. 'It's just that I always drop them off at bingo on a Saturday night.'

'Course not,' I replied, with a tight smile. But even from where I was standing I could see that Tony's mother Iris was already scrutinising me, stripping me right down to the bone. I steeled myself as I shut the front door behind me.

Dutifully, I got into the back of Tony's car. There was obviously a pecking order involved, so I sat next to his father Bernard and made polite chit-chat in the back. We dropped them off at bingo but promised to pick them up later.

We duly picked them up after our date and, as we headed back to my house at the end of the evening, Iris suddenly piped up in the front seat. 'Let's all go for a drink,' she suggested.

Moments later, we pulled up outside the local pub. Once inside, Iris and I found a table and Tony asked what we all wanted to drink.

'An orange juice please,' I replied.

Iris looked at me disapprovingly; she was having none of it. 'An orange juice!' she exclaimed. 'You can't keep drinking orange juice! You need to let your hair down every once in a while. Have a gin in it. Gin and orange, now that's a nice drink.'

I did as I was told and drank a gin and orange. It was the most disgusting thing that I had ever tasted. Needless to say, I haven't touched a drop of gin since.

But his mother wasn't finished with me. Sipping at her own gin and orange, she sniffed and – in her best posh accent – said, 'If you hadn't been the type of girl that we wanted for our Tony, then we'd have done our best to make life as uncomfortable as possible for you.'

I wasn't quite sure how to reply.

'As it is,' she continued, prodding her bony finger against my shoulder, 'you were scrutinised long before you got in the car that day.'

It turned out she'd been asking lots of people questions about me as soon as she found out I was dating her son. She wanted to know if I was a suitable candidate. I looked back at her in astonishment. I'd only met her son twice. Who was to say that our relationship would last any longer? I knew from that moment on that Iris was a tough cookie and that if I wanted to be with her son then I had my work cut out.

Tony also owned a motorbike, and, one evening, he rode over on it to pick me up from work. It was a bitterly cold night, so cold that everything from grass to pavement was covered in a hard silvery glaze of frost. I was due to stay at Tony's house for the weekend but I wasn't dressed for the weather. I was wearing a thin coat, top, skirt and sheer tights. The wind cut through me like a knife as we scooted along the icy roads and back to Tony's house. By the time we arrived, I was so cold that I couldn't climb off – my legs were literally frozen against the seat – still bent at the knee. Tony was laughing as I tried to get off but it took me several minutes just to straighten up!

When we finally walked into his house, Iris was waiting for us and she was furious that Tony had been out on his bike in such bad conditions.

'What's she doing here?' she demanded, pointing at me. 'I've told you a million times before about risking your life for other people.'

I loved Tony's mum in many ways, but whatever I did she always saw me as the woman who would steal away her son, the apple of her eye, the centre of her universe. If I'd been a saint, I still wouldn't have been good enough for her boy.

Tony and I had been dating for just over a year. One Saturday afternoon, we were walking past a jeweller's shop when I felt a tug against my arm. Tony grabbed my hand in his and led me towards the large shop window.

'Here, Jacqui,' he said, 'I want to show you something.'

My eyes darted across the rows and rows of gold rings. Jewels of every size and description glinted in the bright sunlight. Tony pointed through the glass towards a modern-style ring with a huge solitaire diamond set on a square base. The precious stone was nestled on a raised golden shoulder studded with little diamond chippings. It looked expensive.

'Do you like that one?' asked Tony.

'It's lovely,' I said, not quite catching the tone of his voice or realising what he was inferring.

'Let's go in and try it on,' he suggested.

My heart beat in my chest as Tony led me inside. I'd never been in a jeweller's shop as posh as this one and I was worried that my nerves would reveal my inexperience and tender age. But, as soon as I slipped the ring on my finger, everything felt perfect.

'You really like it?' Tony asked me.

'I love it,' I smiled.

'Well, I'm going to buy that ring for you and then perhaps we could get married.'

With that, he took out the wallet from his inside jacket pocket and began to pay.

I stood there dumbfounded. Was that a marriage proposal?

As I watched Tony count out more than a month's salary on to the counter in front of me, I knew that it certainly was.

The male shop assistant smiled knowingly as Tony told him to put it in a box. It would be packed away for later until he could summon up enough courage to tell his mother. All the way home from town in his car, Tony fretted about what to say. How would he tell Iris that he was about to leave home and become a married man? Meanwhile, I was worried how she would react towards me.

When we arrived back at Tony's, Iris was sitting in her usual chair by the fireplace. We began to make small talk about the weather, then suddenly Tony stood up and cleared his throat. I watched as he nervously took the ring box out of his jacket pocket and then I noticed that his hands were shaking slightly.

'I've got something to show you, Mum,' he said, turning towards her with the open box in the palm of his hand. 'I've asked Jacqui to be my wife.'

The room fell into a deep silence. No one spoke as the words hung in the air between the three of us. His mother's face was a picture – she was struck dumb by the news. But there was very little she could do about it other than smile. After all, she had guessed that her son had already spent a month's wages on my ring.

'Ooh, that's nice,' she said, trying to muster up some enthusiasm. She cast her beady eyes over the expensive ring, which was still perched in its box.

'Mind you,' she said, turning her attentions to me, 'you can't have it yet because it wouldn't be proper, not until you've formally announced your engagement.'

So we did. We became officially engaged on 16 May – it was the day of my 17th birthday and the day that I got to wear my ring for the very first time.

Eventually, Iris warmed to the idea of having me as a daughter-in-law and gave us her blessing. The wedding date was set for 27 April 1963. My dream had finally come true.

It was a beautiful crisp spring day when I walked into St Mary's parish church, in Bulwell, Nottingham, to become Tony's wife. It was one of the happiest days of my life.

As my parents were divorced and I hardly ever saw my father, it was decided that my grandfather George would give me away. Proudly, he guided me down the aisle towards my husband. Even though my mother was a single parent, she gave me the best wedding day a bride could wish for. She had bought my wedding dress from a designer she worked with. It was white brocade with a double skirt leading to a long train. It had long white sleeves that led to a neat little point over the back of my hands. They fastened around the wrist with tiny looped brocade-covered buttons. The same buttons ran down the length of the dress at the back. It was simply beautiful.

It was all I'd ever wanted – to be married, go on to have a family of my own and be a good mother to my children. But Iris couldn't help herself – she had to get in just one more dig.

As we left the wedding reception full of excitement and about to embark on our new life together, I heard a lone voice start up at the back. It was Iris – she was singing. Everyone turned to look in astonishment as her voice carried loud and clear across the function room.

'Oh! Oh! Antonio,
'He's gone away,
'Left me alone-ee-o,
'All on my own-ee-o.'

She wailed the chorus again and again in her loudest voice. My mother was mortified and later gave her a piece of her mind. Meanwhile, I wondered what my new life had in store for me.

Tony's dad Bernard was the manager of a chain of mini-market shops. He had heard through the grapevine that a flat above one of the shops was coming up to let. It was small and cramped, with only one bedroom, but it was perfect for a newlywed couple looking for a starter home.

A few months later, we were thrilled to discover I was pregnant with our first child. I sailed through the pregnancy and, as if to perfect the dream, on our first wedding anniversary our beautiful son was born. We named him Mark Anthony Aram.

He was two weeks over his due date but he was long and thin, weighing in at 6lbs 5oz. Back then, this was considered to be just over premature-baby weight. But, at 22 inches long, our son was destined to be as tall as his father.

The birth had been horrendous. The nurses had approached me earlier with a glass and insisted that I drink a foul concoction of orange juice and cod liver oil to bring on the labour. I held my nose as the oily acidic mixture slid down my throat. I don't know how I kept it down – I had to stop myself from gagging as I swallowed. But, as soon as I held my baby boy in my arms, all of that was forgotten.

Tony was desperately waiting for news back home. In those days, men were not allowed to be at the birth of their children. Instead, they were sent for once everything was over and the baby had been cleaned up and was ready to be presented to its father.

I was 18 years old when I had Mark – in many ways still a child – but now I was beginning a new chapter in my life as a mother.

The three of us soon became a happy family unit. I had already decided when I was pregnant that I would give up my work as a hairdresser and concentrate on being the best mum that I could possibly be.

I adored being a mother and everything that went with it. I breastfed Mark, even though it was fashionable back then to put your baby on the bottle. I'd also sing lullabies to him until he drifted off to sleep. Sometimes I'd just sit quietly, holding him in my arms, watching him sleep. I'd stare at him for hours, drinking in each and every one of his perfect little features. I could hardly believe that he was mine to keep. Motherhood had exceeded my expectations so much so that I decided that we should have another child as soon as possible. I wanted my children to be close so we started trying for another baby.

We didn't have to wait long. When Mark was a couple of years old, I discovered I was expecting again. I was careful that Mark wouldn't get jealous or feel pushed out in anyway, so I involved him at every opportunity. As my body began to swell with the new life growing inside it, I would take Mark's tiny hand in mine and place it flat against my stomach. At first, the baby's kicks would make Mark jump back in astonishment but soon he loved to 'feel' the baby.

'Is that my baby brother or sister in there?' he asked, wide-eyed with wonder.

'Yes, sweetheart, it is.'

After that, every time the baby kicked or moved, Mark would be at my side.

'Is the baby saying hello?' he asked one afternoon.

'It is,' I replied.

'Is it today that we are having our new baby, Mummy?'

'No, not today, Mark, but very soon.'

By this time, we'd moved into a smart little bungalow. Months of dragging Mark's heavy pushchair had put an end to our days in the little flat above the shop.

In February, I went out shopping with a friend. I'd felt a little odd all day as we walked around browsing at clothes on rails, and, by the afternoon, I felt even odder.

'I'm sorry,' I told my friend, 'but I think I'm going to have to go home now.'

I started to walk home with Mark in his pushchair. The walk into the small town had been downhill all the way, so, of course, getting home was a different matter – all uphill. I had to keep stopping as I puffed and panted for breath, and I was relieved when we finally made it through the front door.

As the evening progressed, I began to feel pain. There was a tightening across my stomach and contractions. By the early hours of the morning, the pain was so excruciating that I called the midwife, who came to check on me.

'Jacqui, I can't believe you've been out shopping – you're in labour!' the midwife exclaimed.

Tony took Mark next door to keep him out of the way and, a few hours later, our beautiful daughter Colette was born. She weighed more than Mark – a healthy 7lbs 15oz, her skin was olive and she had a shock of black hair. She was just like a baby doll – perfect in every way.

When Mark was brought home, as soon as he saw her, his face lit up with wonder. 'Is that my baby, Mummy?' he gasped, running over to the cot where his little sister was sleeping soundly.

I smiled and nodded. 'This is your sister Colette,' I told him.

'I finally got my baby today!' he cheered, dancing around the room. 'I love her so much, Mummy. I love her and I will always look after her.'

It was a promise Mark would keep – from that moment on, the two of them were always as close as they had been in that special shared moment.

Tony came back into the room. We smiled as Colette nestled peacefully in my arms. Her warm little body rested against my heart linked together forever by an invisible chain of love.

Colette's hair remained dark and glossy – just like her father's – and her huge expressive eyes were the colour of dark almonds. She was as pretty as a picture and adored by everyone who saw her.

As they grew, Mark and Colette remained as close as the day she was born. Mark was always very protective of his little sister. It was as though he saw it as his job to look after her – to keep her from harm. They would walk to the local primary school holding hands, Mark guiding Colette every step of the way.

I refused to have a babysitter – they were my children and far too precious to be left with just anybody.

Instead, we did everything together as a family. The school was only at the end of the road but, as an over-protective mother, I insisted on walking them. But, as they grew, I knew it was time to start loosening the apron strings, and they began demanding to walk there together. I gave in and allowed it, but I still stood watching from the front doorstep. Sometimes I had to pinch myself – how had I produced such wonderful, caring children?

Of course, they weren't perfect. Like any brother and sister, they would often argue and fall out with one another. If Mark was watching a boring programme on TV, Colette would giggle and tease him until he got fed up and left the room; that way, she could switch to a channel she wanted to watch. She was also a real practical joker and was always winding her brother up.

Colette adored Mark and would often hang on his every word, but sometimes it was just comedy. One day, when Mark was eight years old, I was cooking in the kitchen and the children were eating at the table. Mark had obviously had a full day of learning at school and was bursting to share his newfound knowledge with his little sister.

As they ate their tea, Mark decided to impart some of his wisdom. 'Colette, you know the eggs that you eat for breakfast?'

As usual, Colette stopped mid-mouthful to listen to him, and nodded attentively.

'Well, they haven't been fergalised...' he explained.

Colette, not wanting to appear less sophisticated than

him at five years old, nodded wisely. 'Yes,' she said, all matter of fact, 'I know.'

She didn't have a clue what he was talking about (neither did I for that matter. Later we worked out he meant 'fertilised'), but I had to clasp my hand across my mouth to stop myself from crying with laughter.

The children were quite a team when they put their heads together about something, and they constantly nagged me about getting a dog of their own. I wasn't so sure but I relented when my mum bought them a gorgeous Cavalier King Charles Spaniel. She'd taken them to the local breeding kennels in Stanton on the Wolds, and they picked out the pup that they'd loved the best.

By the time they arrived home, Colette was fit to burst with excitement. 'We're calling him Brandy,' she announced as they ran through the door to tell me the news.

Mark was equally thrilled but Brandy was too young to leave his mother, so it was a few more weeks until we were able to go back to the kennels to collect him. Colette was so desperate to bring the dog home that she counted down every single day.

At that time, we had a huge back garden. I've always had a passion for cooking and I use fresh ingredients wherever I can, so I'd insisted that we have our own vegetable patch to grow fresh produce. The garden had a long strip of grass outside the back door, separated by a trellis which gave way to my hallowed vegetable patch. The soil was dark and rich and harboured carrot and runner bean plants. I also had a series of fruit trees, including raspberries and blackcurrants, and nestled right in the middle were my beloved strawberry plants. I lovingly tended them, watering them religiously day and night. The children would look on but I wouldn't let them taste the fruit until it was ready to pick.

One day, all the ripened strawberries were missing when I went to pick them. It was a mystery. After that, it kept happening. When asked, Mark and Colette denied eating them, yet every time the plants were due to ripen, the berries would mysteriously disappear. I began to think that we had a poacher sneaking into the garden at nightfall. It was a complete mystery until one afternoon when the children caught the culprit red-handed – a shame-faced Brandy, tucking into the crop straight from the plants. The brown and white fur around his mouth was stained bright red with sweet, sticky strawberry juice!

As the children became more independent, I decided that I would take a part-time job to make life easier and help pay towards a few luxuries such as school trips and holidays abroad. I also wanted to be a good mum and be there for them. So I planned my working day accordingly. I would work in a local hairdressing salon three days a week until 3.30pm, but I'd always be there when Mark and Colette came home from school at 4pm.

With less of me around, Mark and Colette got their heads together again and hatched a plan to go horse riding. It wasn't cheap but I was steamrollered into letting them go.

'I'll speak to Dad,' I promised, but they already knew that they'd won me over.

Tony agreed, and soon they were going for their first lesson. They took to it like ducks to water.

'Look at them,' I commented to Tony, as we stood proudly watching them. 'You wouldn't get me up there in a month of Sundays, but they look so comfortable – they're naturals.'

And it was true, they were. Soon the children looked forward to their Saturday-morning horse-riding lessons. I wanted to give them a perfect childhood filled with lots of happy memories, as far removed from my own as I could get.

On the way home in the car, Mark and Colette would compare notes and chat about the lesson. Listening to their excited chatter and looking at the joy on their little faces made my heart swell with pride.

Soon the children were experts at riding. At that time the stable owner, Bob Humphries, had decided to introduce jousting. The children were too young to take part but we would all go as a family to watch the instructors dressed in their heavy and cumbersome chain armour suits, a look of determination on their faces as they tried to knock their opponents from the rival horse.

We now seemed to be eating, sleeping and breathing horse riding. But, like all good things, it came to an end. One Saturday morning we took them along and we were told that they were ready to start competing at show jumping.

'Soon, they'll be able to compete in gymkhanas,' the instructor enthused.

I heard Mark sigh heavily behind me. He wasn't keen. 'I just want to ride, Mum,' he said. 'I don't want to do any competitions.'

He was worried that he would be forced to do something that he really didn't want to do, and, by the end of the lesson, his mind was made up. Mark decided he didn't want to go riding any more, and told me so in the car on the way home.

I glanced over at Colette, who was unusually quiet. 'And what do you want to do, love?' I asked.

'Er, I'll try it and see how I get on,' she said, but it was obvious that, without her big brother at her side, the magic had gone.

Colette did return the following Saturday, but without Mark it wasn't the same and she decided that she didn't want to go back.

When Mark was 12, the children's beloved dog Brandy passed away. They missed him, especially Colette, who was broken-hearted. In the end, the following Christmas, we decided to buy her a little Yorkshire terrier, which she called Mitzy. Soon she and Mitzy were inseparable and went everywhere together.

From the age of ten, Colette followed in my footsteps quite literally and took up ballroom dancing along with ballet and tap. Soon she was entering competitions in outfits made by my mother, who was such a talented dressmaker. Over the years, thanks to Mum's dazzling outfits and her own talents, Colette won several medals and diplomas, all of which took pride of place on our mantelpiece at home.

During the long, warm summer holidays, we would pack up the car, drive to the east coast with Mitzy in tow and stay in my mother's bungalow in Mablethorpe, Lincolnshire. By this time, Mum had remarried, to a man called Ron Twells. It was good to see her happy once more. When Tony and I had to return to work, my mum and stepfather would look after the kids at the bungalow so they could enjoy the rest of their school break.

Despite the fact that my mum and dad had divorced years earlier, we were still on good terms with his sister, my aunt May. She and her husband Ken lived in London and we would travel down as a family to stay with them for long weekends. Ken and May were childless and so looked upon Mark and Colette as the closest thing they had to a family of their own. They adored the children and would spoil them with gifts. Colette and Mark loved to stay with them in London, and it wasn't long before they soon made friends with other children in that neighbourhood. To them, it was home from home and they never got tired or bored of going down to visit.

Eventually, May and Ken sold their bungalow in London, and decided to move up north to be closer to us. They found a lovely property in Keyworth, Nottingham, just a stone's throw from where we lived at the time. We were delighted.

'This way we can see more of the children,' May told me.

I was thrilled to have them close by and they soon became very important in all our lives.

The children would nag me to go on school trips and, providing the money was there, I let them. Although money was often tight, Tony and I always tried to give them as much as we could afford. We also had a strict rule – we would never give to one without giving to the other. Everything was fair and equal, as it should be.

'There's no price on a life of happy memories,' I insisted.

It was true; I wanted my children to experience all the wonderful places in the world that I could only dream of going to.

Both children went on exchange trips to France and then, in return, the children they had visited would come and stay with us in England, which was always an experience.

Once Mark had a French pen pal called Eric come to stay during the summer months. Eric was tall and slender with a nest of tight curly blond hair. He was a nice, polite boy but he also had very peculiar eating habits.

One Sunday, we sat down to a full roast dinner with all the trimmings. Yorkshire puddings, mashed potato, beef and roast potatoes all jostled for position on the plates and everything was covered in rich dark gravy.

But Eric wasn't happy. 'Do you have any mayonnaise?' he asked politely.

I looked at him blankly. 'Um, yes, somewhere,' I replied. 'Why?'

'Because I always have mayonnaise with my dinner,' he explained.

The children sat open-mouthed as I went to the kitchen cupboard and retrieved a jar of mayonnaise from the back. We all watched as Eric pulled out a huge spoonful and proceeded to coat his entire dinner with the stuff.

I gave Colette a stern look across the table. She was pulling a face of disgust but I could also see that she was about to collapse into a fit of giggles at any moment. She saw me and looked back towards her own plate and kept quiet.

After that, Eric demanded mayonnaise with every meal – it didn't matter if the food was already covered in thick gravy or tomato sauce, he just had to have it. In the end, I got so fed up of fetching the darn thing from the kitchen that I left the jar permanently on the dining table. It remained there throughout his fortnight's stay.

Colette had a particularly lovely pen pal called Therese and the two became great friends. They wrote to each other for years and remained very close long after their exchange trips.

When the kids weren't at school, they would play with friends at their houses or in our back garden. It was the unwritten rule that I always knew where they were – I didn't want my children roaming the streets. I always liked to know that they were happy and safe.

Besides dancing, my other great passion was cooking. I'd often be found in the kitchen surrounded by children baking cakes and buns, with flour and icing sugar spilled over the floor and every available kitchen surface. Colette and Mark loved to cook too, so I would often hold baking sessions in the kitchen. My friend Sue Copley lived two doors away. Sue didn't like to bake, so I'd invite her two children Melanie and Jason to come over too. Jason and Mark would stand on one side with Colette and Melanie on the other. It would be girls versus boys in the bake-off stakes and, after watching my demonstration, they couldn't wait to get stuck in themselves. Colette's cakes were always the best of the group – she just had a natural talent.

After a while, the other children tired of cooking, but not Colette. She kept it up and would bake for Tony, Mark and me. When I was younger, my father refused to eat anything that I'd cooked, so it was important to me to recognise and give encouragement when the children made us things. I would insist that we would all sit down as a family to taste whatever Colette had made that day. Sometimes the food wasn't very appetising – particularly when she tried to experiment with different herbs and spices – but whatever Colette made, be it a cake, a tart or a simple hot pan of fresh soup, we'd always praise her for her efforts. It also made her happy to see the pleasure in other people's faces as they tucked into something she'd lovingly prepared.

Sometimes I'd catch myself in this happy family scene. I was living in a perfect bubble in the middle of my dream. I was blessed with a lovely family and an adoring husband – what more could anyone want? We had so much fun together – they were the happiest days of my life, if only I could turn the clock back to those precious moments, rewind and live through them just one more time.

The years flew by and soon the children had grown into teenagers. Before long, it was time for Mark and then Colette to sit their exams.

Mark had always wanted to work with electrics. He worked hard and was lucky to secure an apprenticeship at Blackburn and Starling, a local electrician firm.

Colette had it in her mind to become a nurse. She was such a caring girl so it was a natural progression for her to want to do such a worthy job. She spoke to her teacher at school and was sent on work experience at Saxondale Hospital, just outside Nottingham. In those days, it was a mixed hospital but it also had a psychiatric unit, which treated people who had suffered nervous breakdowns. I worried about her safety but Colette gently reminded me that this would be exactly the environment that she would be asked to work in when she became a nurse. However, when she returned home after her first day, she seemed somewhat down in the mouth.

'What's the matter, love? Didn't you enjoy it?' I asked.

Colette shook her head sadly. 'No it's not that, Mum, I loved it, but I've been told that I can't study to become a nurse until I'm at least 18.'

Colette was 15 years old and three more years seemed like a lifetime away to her. She was heartbroken but she also didn't want to wait.

'If I can't be a nurse, then I'll try my second option,' she announced.

'What's that?' I asked.

'A hairdresser, like you, Mum.'

I had mixed feelings about Colette following in my footsteps. Hairdressing wasn't all glamour; it was long hours, standing on your feet all day. But I also didn't want to discourage her from doing something that she really wanted to do.

'Well, if you're sure,' I said.

'I'm sure,' she grinned, wrapping her arms around my neck and giving me a hug.

We lived in Keyworth, Nottingham, and in the middle of the village was a parade of shops – one was a hairdresser called Salvatore. It was run by a wonderful, flamboyant Italian of the same name. Salvatore took to Colette immediately and offered her an apprenticeship starting the following year, when she had finished her school exams. I have never seen my daughter more thrilled. What's more, she'd won it entirely on her own merits.

That September in 1982, Tony and I decided to go to the South of France for a two-week break. Mark was almost 17 years old by then and decided that he was far too grown up to go on holiday with his parents.

'No way!' were his exact words. He stayed at home and my mum, aunt May and uncle Ken popped in every day to check that he was OK.

In the meantime, we enjoyed our fortnight's holiday with Colette and her school friend Amanda. We had no idea at the time, but it would be the last holiday we would ever share with our treasured Colette. For two weeks, we were blissfully happy, unaware of the horrors that were yet to come.

We stayed in an apartment in Cap d'Agde, then a new and up-and-coming resort, a five-hour train ride from Paris and just a few miles from Montpellier. It boasted its own beautiful manmade marina, which moored some of the biggest yachts I'd ever seen. We would walk along there most evenings to have our dinner at one of the little restaurants situated on the waterfront, close to the harbour.

During the day, Tony and I would laze on the beach while the girls went off to explore. On one of the first days, Colette and Amanda ran back along the beach with something to tell us, but they collapsed with a fit of giggles and couldn't talk straight away. After a while, they calmed down enough to tell us what was so funny.

'You're never going to believe it,' exclaimed Colette, 'but there are loads of people down there a bit further along the beach and they've got no clothes on – not a stitch!'

Amanda looked at me and nodded in confirmation.

'What!' I gasped.

'It's true, Mum. There are men along there playing badminton but they're not wearing any clothes – everything is just … well, it's just bobbing about!'

With that, she started laughing again, unable to control herself. Amanda joined in, and the two of them had tears rolling down their cheeks.

'Never!' I said, covering my open mouth with my hand.

'If you don't believe me, then come and have a look for yourself,' Colette insisted.

We walked along the beach for a few minutes until we wandered deep into the group of naturists. Sure enough, they were all naked. Most were men and they were all playing badminton!

'See,' Colette whispered. 'Now do you believe me?'

At that moment, a man walked towards us with his little dog. Colette covered her mouth and buried her head deep into my shoulder to stifle her laughter. The man had the brightest carrot-ginger hair I'd ever seen. He was thin, with a puny physique and he was naked – his bluey-white skin almost glowed in the bright sunshine. He stood out like a sore thumb against the other bronzed naturists. The man was completely starkers apart from a pair of sad-looking sandals that flapped against his feet. A thin brown lead fell limply from his hand and was attached to a little yappy dog with white and ginger fur.

'Look,' said Colette through snorts of laughter, 'they match!'

Soon Amanda, Colette and I were laughing so much that some of the naturists had put down their badminton racquets and had begun to look over at us. We turned and beat a hasty retreat along the shoreline and back to the safety of Tony and the sun loungers.

Lying in the sun wasn't enough for the girls, and they wanted to try their hand at windsurfing. One day, Tony and I paid for them to have a go. I can still picture Colette as she tried to stand up on the board, laughing so much that she would send herself slipping off it and into the sea. Then, despite herself, she would haul herself up and try once more – most of the time she couldn't get back on to the board for laughing. We were in hysterics just watching her from the comfort of our sun loungers.

Colette saw us and ran back on to the beach. 'I'm

exhausted,' she said, flopping down on a nearby towel, baked warm and dry from the hot midday sun.

'You're quite the expert,' I teased.

Colette rolled her eyes and laughed. Once she was dry, she ran back into the sea towards Amanda with her board to have another go.

She spent more time in the water than the windsurfing board itself. It still makes me smile to think of her happy in the sunshine, free from cares and worries – two weeks of bliss, never wanting to return home.

But return home we did, and Colette was due to start her final year at school before she embarked on her new and chosen career.

A few months later, in January, the phone rang. It was Salvatore, who wanted Colette to go and see him at the salon. We were puzzled as she wasn't due to start her apprenticeship until the summer.

Less than an hour later, Colette walked in through the front door. She was in floods of tears and was inconsolable.

'Whatever's the matter?' I asked, holding her in my arms. I'd never seen her so upset.

It took a few minutes for Colette to compose herself. Her chest was heaving with big heavy sobs, as through her tears she began to explain that Salvatore had decided that he was going to sell the hairdressing salon.

'So there's going to be no apprenticeship, no position and no hairdressing job for me,' she sobbed.

'It'll be OK,' I soothed.

But Colette's heart was broken. To her this was

the end of the world, and she fled to her bedroom, shutting the door behind her. But hours later, despite my assurances that something would come up, I could still hear her crying.

The following morning at breakfast, I tried to speak to her. 'Colette, you've got a while before you finish school – at least six months, something else will come up.'

But she was barely listening; she was devastated. First the nursing and now this. I didn't know what to do to make it better.

Later that day, Colette went to visit May and Ken in a bid to cheer herself up. She told them what had happened at the salon and how Salvatore was selling up. She was still feeling fed up when she came home a few hours later.

A few days later, I dropped by to see Ken and May. We were discussing Colette's predicament and I told them how upset she had been. 'I've never seen her like this – it's as though the wind has been stolen from her sails,' I sighed.

Aunt May thought for a while. 'How about we buy the salon and then Colette can have her apprenticeship?' she suggested.

I looked at her in astonishment. 'No,' I said. 'You can't do that – it's too much, it'll cost a fortune.'

But May was adamant and so was Ken. Colette and Mark were the closest thing they had to children of their own, so why not let them help out and keep it in the family? As it turned out, they'd already decided and had made the necessary enquiries. They had it all worked out.

'I could manage it,' May explained, 'Ken can do the

maintenance on the shop, you can work there and Colette can have her apprenticeship after all. It's perfect. Then, when she's fully trained, we could give her the salon – it would secure her future.'

Ken nodded in agreement. 'We've been looking for an investment,' he said, 'and this is it.'

And so it was decided. All we had to do now was tell Colette.

That teatime, when I returned back home, Colette was mooching around the house – she'd been like that since she'd received the news about the job.

'Aunt May and Uncle Ken are popping by to see you later,' I called to her.

'Why?' she asked.

'Oh, I don't know. They want to see you about something,' I said, trying not to give too much away in my voice. It was Ken and May's job to deliver the exciting news.

Shortly afterwards, there was a knock at the door. It was my aunt and uncle. We called Colette down and she glumly walked into the front room. Her face was still crushed with the disappointment of the week before.

'Aunt May and Uncle Ken have something to tell you,' I began.

Colette looked at them quizzically.

'We're buying you the salon; that way you can have your apprenticeship and eventually run the shop!' May told her.

Colette's mouth fell open in disbelief. She gasped and clasped her hand over her mouth. Her brown eyes lit up with excitement, as she looked from Ken and May to me.

I nodded. 'It's true, what do you think?' I said.

'Really? That's brilliant!' Colette gasped, running over to hug them. Her eyes were full of tears but this time they were tears of joy.

'I just can't believe it. Thank you. Thank you so much,' Colette said again and again.

At last, my daughter's future was secure, or so we thought. After that moment, Colette was back to her old self. She was excited and was looking forward to starting her new career.

Salvatore sanctioned the sale and, as part of the deal with May and Ken, it was agreed that Colette would help out after school and on Saturdays. She began her training. She did everything from taking phone calls to making tea and coffee. If she wasn't sweeping up hair from the floor, she'd be at the sink shampooing customers. She loved every minute and relished every moment in her new role.

One of the benefits of being a teenage girl working in a hairdressers was that Colette also got to try out all the new hairstyles for free. One day, she returned home from work and shot past me quickly in the hallway. She had her head bowed and I was immediately suspicious.

'Wait a minute, young lady,' I said. 'What's that at the front of your hair?'

As Colette turned to face me, I gasped. The front of her beautiful dark glossy hair had been bleached within an inch of its life. In its place was an awful custard-coloured yellow fringe the texture of frazzled straw!

'Oh, Colette,' I sighed, 'What have you done?'

But Colette remained defiant. 'I like it,' she sniffed.

I shook my head. It looked awful. 'Colette, it looks horrible, like a line across the front of your head. You've got lovely hair – you don't need to do that to it.'

But Colette insisted that the custard-coloured fringe was here to stay. 'It's fashion, Mum,' she said.

'Well, if that's fashion, you can keep it.' I retorted. 'It looks, well, really cheap – and you're not cheap, Colette. Please dye it back again.'

I was begging her but she was already halfway up the stairs.

'I'm in hairdressing, Mum,' she said crossly. 'What do you expect?' With that she slammed her bedroom door.

In April, we celebrated Mark's 19th birthday. Most people gave him money because boys that age are hard to choose presents for. Mark decided to buy a dog with his cash. He was working by now, so I reasoned he could afford to keep his own dog. He went to some kennels nearby and soon returned with a gorgeous Old English sheepdog.

'I'm calling her Zara,' he told us.

Colette adored Zara and was always making a fuss of the dog. She still had the hated hairstyle but I was working slowly to convince her to dye it back to its natural state.

A few days later, Colette was playing with Zara when Mark picked up the camera from the side unit. 'Here, let's get a photograph,' he said.

Colette momentarily looked up; Mark pressed the button and the shutter snapped shut. There she was happy and smiling, frozen in time, frozen in that moment forever and ever. Little did I know then that this was to be the last ever photograph taken of my beautiful daughter and one that I would treasure during the long torturous years that followed. How I have wanted to pluck Colette from it and pull her back into my arms. I have held it to my heart countless times. It is my most treasured possession.

At 16, Colette was a child in a growing woman's body. She held the innocence and untarnished optimism of a child. She'd spent her entire life surrounded by love and she in turn loved those who surrounded her. She'd never been exposed to violence or horror and therefore trusted others – she thought everyone was as lovely and pure as she was. She loved life and, in turn, it loved her back.

We'd protected her all her life: she was her father's little princess, Mark's wonderful younger sister and my angel – an extension of me – she held my heart and soul in her hands. Colette brought a bright, warm and wonderful light into our lives. Unbeknown to us, that vibrant light was about to be extinguished forever.

CHAPTER 2

THE NIGHTMARE
BEGINS

It was the day before Halloween – 30 October 1983. I
pulled open the curtains and squinted in the unexpected
sunlight. The day was bright and full of hope. I looked at
the trees outside. The golden light of early morning filtered
through the branches into my bedroom. It was a glorious
crisp Sunday morning, unusual for the time of year.

I heard Mark and Colette stirring, so I pulled on my
slippers and dressing gown and headed down for
breakfast. Tony had a lie-in, while I busied myself making
a cooked breakfast for me and the children.

It was a typical weekend; everyone had plans for the
day ahead. Mark was going to see a friend, while Tony
and I were due to visit nearby relatives. Colette had
arranged to see her boyfriend later that evening.

'Do you want to come with me and Dad?' I asked
Colette as she picked at her poached egg on toast.

'No, Mum, I'll just stay here. I want to bake a cake, so I'll do that instead. You can have it for your tea,' she smiled.

That afternoon, Tony and I left home around 2.30pm and drove the short distance to see May and Ken. It was an afternoon of small talk but we also spent time discussing Ken's elderly mother's deteriorating health.

By the time we returned, it was 5pm, just in time for tea. Colette was busy clearing up in the kitchen. As soon as I walked in the front door, I smelled the delicious aroma of home cooking. I gasped when I saw it taking pride of place on the kitchen worktop – a beautiful Victoria sponge cake oozing with fresh cream and jam. It was cookbook picture perfect.

'Wow, that looks delicious!' I exclaimed.

Colette's face lit up. 'Thanks, Mum!' she beamed. She looked so proud.

I held my hands out and Colette walked towards me, wrapped her arms around me and enveloped me in a hug. It always felt so good to hug my precious, beautiful girl.

Colette was a great cook. She took pride in her work and insisted on cleaning up the kitchen before getting ready for her date with her boyfriend Russell Godfrey.

Russell and Colette had been dating for about eight months. Russell was 17 – a year older than Colette – but he was a kind and gentle boy, the type every mother would want for their daughter.

Russell would usually drive over and pick Colette up in his silver Vauxhall. He was one of the few boys his age to have already passed his test and have his own car. Then again, his parents did run the local driving school. The family had a fleet of cars, but they were all at the garage that night. As a result, Russell had no transport.

At 7.45pm, Colette came downstairs and grabbed her coat. She'd spent time blow-drying her hair – it was dark and glossy and styled in a neat cropped cut. Colette was trying out different looks as teenage girls do. She had such a pretty little face that, whatever she did, she always looked lovely.

While Colette was still fussing over her make-up – she wanted to look her best for Russell – she told me that they planned to watch a video together and maybe go into the village later to meet up with friends.

'I'm off to Russell's now,' she announced suddenly, and gave her mouth one last slick of lipgloss.

I glanced through the window at the inky black sky outside. A silvery hue from an eerie full moon was the only source of light now. The beautiful day had given way to a frosty autumn evening.

'I'll take you in the car,' I said.

'No, Mum, I'd rather walk,' she replied, sliding her arms into her cropped red jacket. She was wearing black corduroy trousers and a white silky blouse underneath. As I glanced at her, I thought how stunning she looked, just like a model.

I glanced anxiously out the window again. It was cold and dark out there and I didn't like the idea of my 16-year-old daughter walking alone.

'Well, if you won't let me take you, let your dad,' I insisted.

But Colette was adamant. 'It's a nice night. I'd rather walk. But, if Russell calls, tell him that I'm going to walk up Nicker Hill.'

Nicker Hill was the main hill leading through the village. It had a fairly steep incline but it was well lit on one side with fields on the other side of the road. I knew that Colette would keep to the well-lit path, as Russell's home was in Willow Brook, which joined that side of the road.

I can't explain it, but I had a knot of anxiety in the pit of my stomach. I simply didn't want her walking the 10 minutes to Russell's house. But what could I do? Colette was an independent 16-year-old; she knew her own mind and didn't want her mother fussing.

Before she left, Colette walked over and said, 'Love you lots and lots.' Then she gave me a kiss.

'Love you too,' I called back as she walked out of the house and closed the front door behind her.

It was 7.50pm when she left.

Russell rang five minutes later. I told him what Colette had said and he set off on his bike to meet her. At 8.10pm, the phone rang again. It was Russell. His voice was breathless and he sounded a little confused.

'Jacqui, I thought you said that Colette had walked up Nicker Hill?'

'I did, Russell – that's what Colette told me.'

'Well,' he said, trying to catch his breath, 'I've cycled all the way around the village and I can't see her anywhere.'

Suddenly, I felt very sick. The knot of anxiety in my stomach had risen through my body and was now lodged as a lump in my throat. On hearing Russell's words, my throat went bone dry and was constricted with panic. I knew in an instant that something was very wrong. Colette was the kind of girl who hated others to worry about her. If she'd stopped off anywhere, she would have phoned to tell us. She knew how worried her father and I would have been.

Colette had left just over ten minutes before but I knew instinctively that she was missing. I put the phone down, took a deep breath, picked the receiver back up and dialled 999.

The police officer on the other end of the line didn't share my concern. 'How can you say a 16-year-old girl is missing at 8pm on a Sunday night?' he scoffed, more than a hint of disbelief in his voice.

'Easy,' I told him, 'because she's my daughter. It's just not like her to vanish like this. I know her.'

Colette had been brought up to respect others. She was a caring girl who wouldn't want to upset or annoy people. She always operated within certain boundaries and would never just decide to take off without telling anyone.

'What time is she usually home at night?' asked the officer. His voice had softened a little. I guess he thought he was dealing with an over-protective mother.

'Around 9.30pm, or just after, but never much later. She knows how much I'd worry.'

The officer thought for a moment and then said, 'Well, I'll tell you what, if she's not home for 10.30pm, just give us another call.'

With that, he hung up.

I was dumbstruck. Instinct told me that something was very wrong, but how could I get the police to take my fears seriously? I knew something had happened to my daughter. I picked the receiver back up and began dialling frantically around all our friends and family to see if they'd seen or heard from Colette. No one had.

I called all the hospitals in the area. Had they admitted a teenage girl? Had Colette been caught up in some dreadful accident? But I got the same answer from every A&E switchboard – there had been no reported accident concerning a girl in or around Keyworth.

By this point, I was crying. Huge teardrops streamed down my face and pooled into my hands.

Tony stood by me, ashen-white. He felt as helpless as I did but tried his best to reassure me. 'Come on, Jacqui. You always think the worst. Everything will be OK,' he soothed.

I wanted to believe him – to think that there was a simple explanation, but there wasn't. I knew my daughter too well. She was my twin – the double of me. Colette wouldn't have just wandered off somewhere on her own at night.

We stood still for a few moments. Suddenly, I said, 'We've got to find her, Tony. She's lying in a hedge somewhere – I know she is.'

The survival instinct kicked into both of us. We jolted into action. As her parents, we could do something about this.

'Let's get the cars and go and look for her,' said Tony.

Soon, we were ringing around asking others to join in

the search for our daughter. If the police wouldn't help us, then we'd do it ourselves.

Tony and I called our neighbour and friend Jan. She was also the acting manageress of the hairdressing salon where Colette worked. Jan and her husband Tony came over to help us look for Colette. My aunt May also drove over in her car. In the middle of all this commotion, Mark arrived home. He was bewildered by my tears and the building sense of panic at home.

'Colette's missing,' I said, tears stinging in my eyes as I mouthed the words, which made it all too real. 'We're all going to look for her.'

'I'll help,' Mark gasped, as he grabbed his car keys and ran back to his parked car on the drive outside.

We all drove towards different parts of the village – it felt good to be proactive – but we couldn't find Colette anywhere. We travelled along the route that she would have taken and beyond, just in case, but there was still no sign of her. It was hopeless.

By 9.30pm, I was frantic and couldn't wait much longer. I rang the police a second time. I was in a state of true panic. My heart thumped so loudly that I thought it would leap out of my chest. I spoke to another police officer who agreed to help me.

'We'll send someone out,' he promised me.

At last, I thought, we'll find her now. But the first officer who knocked at our door told me that he was here to search our loft. 'Just in case,' he reasoned.

'Why on earth would she be in the loft?' I asked, incredulous.

Despite my protests, he strode past me, climbed the stairs and opened up the loft hatch in the landing ceiling. The officer switched on his torch and climbed up awkwardly through it. I watched numbly in disbelief as the light darted around the darkened, empty loft space above.

'Why would she be in the loft?' I repeated, tears of frustration welling up inside me.

This was pointless. We were wasting precious time. Colette could be anywhere, I thought. She could be hurt, crying out for me.

'She left home perfectly happy a few hours ago,' I insisted. This loft 'search' was nonsense.

Moments later, the police officer was back on the landing, dusting himself down. 'Nothing up there but storage boxes,' he agreed, gesturing upwards with his finger.

I was exasperated. Each minute that ticked by was another minute without my daughter, another minute with her further from me and the safety of her family.

The officer radioed the information back to police headquarters, who agreed to send backup. It was midnight by the time four uniformed officers arrived at our home with two sniffer dogs. They planned to walk with the police dogs towards the bottom of Nicker Hill, which was five minutes' walk from our home in Normanton Lane.

'Wait,' I said, grabbing the nearest coat, 'I'm coming with you.'

I pulled on the coat, a thin, lime-green leather-look

raincoat. It was my favourite coat but now it was associated with the horrors of searching for my daughter. I was frozen with both cold and fear as I followed the officers and searched nearby fields.

My mind was racing. I was panic-stricken. My throat was tight and dry and I felt sick as we walked along the darkened road. I kept repeating the same thing to myself over and over again: 'She's lying in a hedge bottom somewhere. She's dead. I just know she is. Colette wouldn't put us through this.'

My teeth chattered with fear as I spoke. My whole body began to shake uncontrollably.

'We must find her. Please, God, help us find my baby,' I kept repeating like a prayer.

I was freezing and crying, unable to get the thought out of my head that Colette was lying dead somewhere. I begged the officers to find her.

Although it was still a full moon, the light had faded hours before, making the search almost impossible.

'We're going to have to stop and continue with it tomorrow,' a senior officer announced. He felt so uncomfortable with his own announcement that he was barely able to look me in the eye.

Then he asked me about Colette's friends. How could I be certain that she hadn't stopped off somewhere? They asked about Colette's friend Sarah Newman, whose parents ran the Golden Fleece pub in Upper Broughton, outside the village.

'Do you think that she might have strolled over there?' the officer asked.

'I am telling you, I know my daughter,' I sobbed. 'There is no way that she would have walked across fields and a motorway to get there. Why would she?'

The police told me to make the call anyway, so I did. It was the early hours of the morning when the phone rang at the Golden Fleece pub, but I remember that call as if it was yesterday. Sarah's mother answered and went to wake her sleeping daughter. But Sarah hadn't seen or heard from Colette that night – it appeared that no one had. It was as though my daughter had simply vanished off the face of the earth.

Instead, weary with both mental and emotional exhaustion, I returned home and hung my damp raincoat back on the cloakroom peg. I never wore my favourite coat again.

By this time, Colette's boyfriend had arrived at our house. Russell was in a dreadful state and wanted to stay with us throughout the night in case we heard any news.

Tony, Mark, Russell and I stood in a daze; the stark kitchen light highlighted the growing fear and worry on our faces. In a matter of hours, we had been drawn into a living nightmare, a torturous waiting game that could not even begin to come to an end until first light.

We did wait. We waited for Colette to walk in the front door. We waited for a phone call that never came. Then, in those last few hours, we sat waiting for the sun to rise once more and cast light on Colette's sudden disappearance.

I heard the sound of a van pull up outside. I dashed to the front door, hoping that it was the police bringing her home. But it was the milkman. It was 5am, and I startled him as I flung open the door to ask if he'd seen Colette.

'She's been missing all night,' I explained, shaking and red-eyed from crying.

The milkman had known Colette since she was a little girl so he knew it was completely out of character for her to go missing. 'That's not like Colette,' he replied, a little shocked. 'But, if I see her, I'll certainly let her know how worried you all are.'

I thanked him for his kindness, but by now I felt dead inside, like all hope had been lost.

I closed the front door wearily and returned to Tony. 'I just know she's dead in a hedge somewhere,' I said, weeping.

Tony had reassured me earlier. But now, the more he thought about it, the more he knew something was very wrong. Eventually, he stopped talking altogether and we all just sat there in silence, numb and shell-shocked.

At 5.45am, I made the call I had been dreading. I called my mother Joyce to tell her that Colette was missing. I could barely get the words out for crying and Mum had to keep asking me to repeat what I was saying. She said she'd be over straight away with my stepfather.

When I saw her car pull up outside, I ran straight to her and, as she held me in her arms, I collapsed in a heap of tears. Everything seemed so surreal. Other people had arrived at our house too. My aunt and uncle, who we'd spent the day before with, turned up along with Russell's parents. They felt dreadful and, like the rest of us, they blamed themselves.

'If only the cars hadn't been off the road,' Russell had said time and time again throughout the night.

His parents stayed for an hour or so but no one knew what to say or think. My mum went into the kitchen to make everyone a cup of tea. I think it was her way of coping; something to occupy her mind, to stop her thinking the worst.

I appreciated everyone's kindness, but I could barely speak to them. Instead, I just sat by the window, waiting for the light to come and bring me my daughter back home.

As soon as dawn broke, Mark and my stepfather Ron went out to continue the search. They were driving past a nearby field off Thurlby Lane, about a mile and a half from our home, when Mark spotted the striped blue tape of a police cordon at the side of a field. His car screeched to a halt. Mark jumped from the car and began running towards the cordoned-off field by the bottom of a hedgerow. As he approached, a police officer tried to hold him back, but it was too late. Mark glanced over the officer's shoulder and saw a sight that will haunt him for the rest of his life.

'That's my sister!' Mark howled, his cries echoing around the deserted farmland.

In front of his eyes lay his frail little sister naked, bruised, battered and dead. My nightmare premonition had come true.

She'd been strangled – the life squeezed out of her innocent and now broken body. She lay like a rag doll, cold and lifeless at the bottom of the hedge, and had been arranged by her killer in a sickening sexually explicit pose. He had even tied her blouse and bra around her wrist as some sort of twisted trophy or calling card.

The horrors of what he saw that day changed Mark in an instant. No brother should have to see his sister like that. My son's life would never be the same again.

Back at home, I remained seated by the front-room window waiting for news. I was as pale and as frozen as a porcelain statue. A police officer had been dispatched to keep guard outside at the end of our drive.

I knew my daughter was dead before my son had even made it through the front door. When Mark and Ron pulled up in the car outside, I instinctively rose from the armchair where I had been sitting. As I did so, I saw the policeman shaking his head sadly, looking towards the house. I knew in that instant that my beautiful Colette had gone.

A scream came from deep within me and it didn't stop. I saw Tony and my mother – their lips were moving but the only sound I could hear was my own desperate screams.

Then Mum picked up the phone and began to dial a number.

My screams didn't stop until the doctor arrived with a couple of needles. He'd come to inject me with a tranquilliser. My eyes glazed over, a kind of numb relief came over me. Zombie like, I was led to bed, where I stayed for the rest of the day until the effects of the drug wore off. Then I was injected again, and again. This pattern of drug-induced numbness continued to keep me in a blurry, semi-detached haze for around ten days. It was meant to protect me from the horror of our reality and to give me time to adjust to the news that I would never see my lovely Colette ever again.

Our nightmare had begun.

CHAPTER 3
THE AFTERMATH

The doctor had filled the syringe with tranquilliser to sedate me. But there was something that I needed to do. I picked up the phone, dialled a number and waited for an answer. Then, in a calm voice, I spoke. 'I'm sorry, but I won't be in to work today because Colette's been murdered,' I said in a monotone voice. I was functioning on auto-pilot. The words came out of my mouth like I was a robot.

At that time, I worked for Lancôme as a beauty consultant in Debenhams department store in the centre of Nottingham. I loved my job and had served everyone from Barbara Windsor to Dale Winton, who at that time was working for the local radio station. He'd always been so polite and lovely towards me. In fact, I had built up a warm and loyal base of customers, so it was a real wrench not to be there and to have simply disappeared overnight.

The company was very good to me and gave me full paid leave to cope with my grief. Each week, a huge box of flowers would arrive for me from my work colleagues. I couldn't have wished to work for better people. As well as flowers, staff and area managers would write and telephone me regularly to check how I was coping. It was beyond the call of duty and I will be forever grateful to those who made those early days so much easier to bear.

One of these people was my mother. For the first two weeks, she moved into our home to cook and clean and generally keep an eye on us all. I couldn't have coped without her strength and support. But, despite all the lovely home-cooked meals she made, I couldn't eat. Instead, I survived the next two weeks on a diet of prescribed tranquillisers and milky drinks. I couldn't even stand food near my mouth; it just made me retch. It seemed wrong somehow to even want to eat – or to live – with Colette cold and dead.

I drank Ovaltine made with milk. I would be just about alert enough for when the GP arrived for his daily visit. He would walk into the house, pull out and prepare a hypodermic needle, stick it into my arm and allow me to drift off into a zombie state once more. While the sedation brought me a sense of calm, I hated the feeling of hardly being able to stand up. I would fall about and sway like someone who had had too much to drink. I just felt hollow inside – like the walking dead. No emotions, no feelings, just complete emptiness.

As word about Colette spread, more and more people arrived at our home with flowers. Soon the house was full to bursting point with different bunches everywhere. They were in the lounge, dining room, kitchen, hallway and they even lined the stairs. A carpet of flora filled every step until we finally ran out of vases – our own and others that we'd had to borrow from neighbours and friends.

But no amount of united grief or compassion would bring my little girl back. Before this nightmare, I'd been a happy, outgoing person. Now I was a shell of my former self. I was shattered, my confidence fragmented into thousands of pieces like a broken mirror, hopeless and waiting to be repaired. All the joy in my life had drained from me the night that Colette died.

The doctor arrived one day and, upon being hit by the overwhelming floral scent filling our home, he reeled back in disgust. Then he began to shout.

'This house is like a shrine,' he exclaimed.

We were dumbstruck, as if life couldn't get any more surreal. We turned to stare at him; he was our doctor, a pillar of the community. He was normally so gentle, professional and cheery. His words had jolted us all.

Then he turned his attentions to me. 'And as for you, Jacqui, if you don't eat soon, I'll be treating you for anorexia.'

I was stunned. The doctor wasn't an unkind man; he was just trying to shock me back to some sort of normality.

'Do you really think Colette would want to see you like this?' he asked, holding up one of my pathetic gaunt arms to inspect. He gestured towards my concave torso with a jab of his hand.

I tried to shrug but I didn't have the energy. I just felt weak, like a battered rag-doll, the stuffing knocked clean out of me.

The doctor turned to Tony and other relatives sat in the room. 'And, while you're at it, get rid of some of these sodding flowers!'

He was right about the flowers, of course. Nothing or no one could pierce the pain of my loss. I also knew that he was saying these things to try to help me, to shock me. But no one could because I didn't want to come back to the normal world and my life as it would now be. I didn't want to eat, to breathe or even to live. I just wanted to die and lie alongside my little girl. To protect her.

Eventually, after a couple of weeks, I refused to let the doctor inject me any more. He insisted that I had some other kind of tranquilliser, this time in tablet form, but he scaled his usual daily visit down to every few days. On the face of things, it looked as if I was coping, working through my loss, but I was far from doing either of these things.

My haze of grief continued as I went into denial that Colette had gone. I would sit by the window or on the chair in the hall, waiting for her to come home. Every day I searched for her outline. At times I thought I saw her but it was always someone else's daughter. I willed her to walk up the driveway and into our home. I pictured her usual smile and cheery 'hiya, Mum', as she strolled in through the front door, hanging her red jacket up on the usual peg.

But there was no outline, no smile, no Colette.

Instead, well-meaning strangers knocked with more condolence cards and more bunches of sodding flowers.

The police came to see us. Someone had to identify Colette's body. They wouldn't let me go as they didn't think that I'd be able to cope with the sight that awaited me at the mortuary. Also, for my own sanity I needed to remember Colette for the beautiful girl she had always been. I didn't want horror visions to seep in and tarnish the happy memories that I held dear in my heart. I didn't want to see my daughter dead and lying alone and lifeless on a mortuary slab.

Instead, Tony and my dad Arthur went to identify her battered body. She was black and blue all over – an alien and broken version of herself.

My father was not a well man. He suffered with angina and other health issues, and he never got over what he saw that day. But somehow he held the hurt and buried it deep down inside. Arthur was a proud man; a strong, hard business man. But the shock of seeing his granddaughter in this state haunted him for the rest of his life. He died broken-hearted less than six months later. He was just 65 years old. Colette's murderer had now claimed two lives. I had saved myself from this horrific vision but the shock had killed my dad. I wondered then how we were supposed to cope in the forthcoming months.

If I did manage to get past the front door, I became too terrified to go back in fearing that her killer was waiting for me. The question of mistaken identity was raised by the police investigation team – it was suggested that I might have been the intended target – so I became a virtual recluse in the sanctuary of my own home and suffered constant panic attacks.

For days, I just drifted in and out of oblivion. I didn't know what day of the week it was, or anything else for that matter – nothing seemed important any more. My baby had gone.

The police had a lead. A car had been stolen from an area five miles south of Nottingham. The red Ford Fiesta had been taken around 4.30pm on the Sunday afternoon – less than four hours before Colette went missing.

The police also informed me that a resident in the area where Colette had walked had heard screams around 8.14pm. The time perfectly matched the moment that my daughter had gone missing. The unnamed resident had looked out and spotted a small car moving off at high speed. It was a red Ford Fiesta.

Days later, I was told that a grief-stricken Russell had placed a notice in the paper to his sweetheart. It read: 'Colette, words cannot express how I feel. I'll never forget you and you will be forever with me in my thoughts. All my love forever, Russell.'

I was grateful for Russell's kind words. It helped me enormously to think that others ached for Colette as much as I did.

Two days after the murder, the police received another strong lead. A landlady from the Generous Briton pub, in the nearby village of Costock, had telephoned them to say that she had served a man who had been acting suspiciously around 9pm on the night of the murder. He was a stranger to her. She served him an orange juice and lemonade, and he also bought a ham sandwich. He then had another half of orange and lemonade from her; she got talking to him and asked why he was in the area that night.

'I've come off the motorway at the wrong junction,' he began, before suddenly changing his story to say he was visiting a friend who'd had an accident.

As he spoke, the landlady glanced down and noticed that this strange man had bloodstains on his hand. He saw her eyes dart from his bloodied hand and back to his face. Suddenly, he withdrew the bloodied hand into the sleeve of his jacket and made a hasty retreat to the pub toilet. The woman heard him wash his hands before drying them with a paper towel. Moments later, he left the pub and disappeared back into the darkened night never to be seen again. When reports of Colette's murder began to appear in the local newspaper and also on the regional TV stations, the landlady, unnerved by what she'd seen, called the police a few days after the murder to tell them all about the suspicious man.

The police went directly to the pub where the landlady recounted the entire story to them. Officers went into the men's toilet to retrieve all the paper towels from the wastepaper bin. Little did we know at this stage, but future advancements in DNA technology – then still in its infancy – would use this vital piece of evidence to eventually nail Colette's killer. The landlady had come face to face with the man who'd killed my daughter. She agreed to help the police by allowing them to bring in a hypnotist so that she could recall the brief encounter in minute detail. The landlady proved to be a brilliant witness and provided the police with lots of information about the man and what he looked like. The police then issued a photofit of this suspect. I hoped and prayed that stopping off for a drink in a pub – as if in celebration of Colette's murder – would be this ruthless killer's undoing.

All the hand towels were sent off for analysis to be expertly examined, but back then, with DNA techniques still in development, all the scientists were able to establish was a blood grouping on one. But, as the techniques became more refined, they were able to unlock more and more DNA from that single towel with which they would eventually pinpoint Colette's killer. That single paper towel was to play an absolutely vital role in the future of the investigation.

The police were also looking at the stolen car. It had been removed and transported to the Home Office Research Unit, based in Sandwich. I was informed that a team of forensic experts were going to carry out a series of tests on the car's interior. If the killer had left his mark, the police would find it.

The following day, an inquest into Colette's death was held at Nottingham Coroner's Court.

A statement was read out from Detective Superintendent Denis Hanley of Nottingham CID. He said Colette's body had been spotted in the field by a passing motorist on the Monday morning – the day after her disappearance. A post-mortem examination had been carried out which revealed that she had died from asphyxia as a result of manual strangulation. Tony was there, and he broke down in tears as he listened to the details.

The inquest was adjourned for the time being. Afterwards, Tony was in such a state that he had to be helped from the court. Meanwhile, I was at home, as I wasn't fit to attend. I was barely able to get up in the morning, never mind show my face in public.

Because of the opening of the inquest into her death, for the first six months we were unable to bury my little girl in case her killer was caught – back then bodies were kept longer so that defence teams could perform their own post mortem. These days more consideration is given to the victim's family and bodies are released quicker.

Colette's body was placed on ice as we waited for an arrest which didn't come.

Every night, I'd climb into bed thinking of my daughter lying in the mortuary. The image haunted me. Although I'd refused to go and see her, I couldn't help wanting to know what my daughter now looked like. Before my father died, I'd needed to ask him what this monster had done to my little girl. He told me that Colette had been peppered with cuts and bruises and was black and blue all over. After hearing my dad's description, this was all I could see in my mind's eye: my baby girl lying in a huge fridge covered in bruises, tinged blue from the cold. I wanted to lie beside her, to die with her. I just wanted to wrap her in my arms and keep her warm. I didn't want her to be alone or feel frightened.

I tried hard to visualise Colette as I wanted to remember her, laughing and joking, lighting up the room with her innocent sweet smile. But, try as I might, I just couldn't shake this horrific new vision from my mind. I tortured myself daily with it until it was all I could think of. I'd now forgotten how to function. My world had become so grim that I allowed the blackness of it to wash over me. I just couldn't get this image of her out of my mind.

Why Colette? Why not me? Was it our fault she was dead? Should we have insisted again and again until she finally agreed to allow one of us to take her to Russell's house in the car? There were so many questions but no answers. All I had was a mountain of grief.

But friends and family helped me through. My good friend Sue Copley was my rock. Sue used to come and sit with me each day. She sat there for so many hours. On the good days, she'd sit and wait in a chair in the front room; on the bad ones, she'd perch herself on my bed, watching, waiting for me to come around.

My mother would come in and sigh sadly when she saw the pair of us. 'She's out of it, Sue. The doctor came and gave her another injection this morning.'

But Sue was adamant that she would wait until I came around. 'I don't care; I'll sit on her bed for as long as it takes. I just need her to know that I am here for her.'

Each time I awoke, Sue would be there for me.

I think I used to feel awkward when people fussed round me because I didn't really know what to say, or what I was expected to say. But Sue never expected anything from me.

Knowing that she was just there for me gave me the strength that I needed to carry on. She was a brilliant friend to me in those early days and still is to this day – the same goes for her husband Pete.

Then the phone calls started.

A girl rang just days after her murder. 'Can I speak to Colette?' she said.

For a moment, the mere mention of my daughter's name took my breath away. Who would ring asking such a question?

'Who is it?' I asked, numb and confused.

'A friend,' the girl said.

'Well, if you're a friend, you will know that she's dead,' I replied, slamming down the receiver.

I remained there, trembling with anger. Why would someone make such a call? Surely they must have known what had happened? Colette's murder was all over the news channels, so much so that I couldn't bear to turn the TV on for fear of seeing her lovely face staring back at me. Now she was public property, hijacked by the media who were eager for updates on the 'murdered teenager'.

After that, every day like clockwork, between 2pm and 3pm, the phone would ring. I would answer it but no one would speak – instead there was just heavy breathing. The calls kept coming for hours. I would shake every time the phone went. I was convinced that it was Colette's killer taunting us, watching on from his secret lair.

One day, someone phoned and asked for Tony. When he

answered, an unknown voice told him that I had sexually transmitted diseases. 'Your wife has venereal disease and syphilis,' mocked the voice. 'You should get yourself tested at the doctors.'

Tony never told me if it was a man or a woman. I never found out why, but I can only guess he was thinking of my fragile state and was acting to protect me.

Why were people intent on being so cruel? What sort of sick mind would want to do this to my family – hadn't we suffered enough?

The phone calls continued every day. It got to the stage that, whenever the phone rang, I would stiffen and freeze to the spot and my whole body would begin to shake. It became a new fear – something else to cope with.

The police thought that the phone calls were all in my mind. As time went on, even my own husband came to disbelieve me. After all, why would someone be so cruel as to torment me every single day? I started to doubt myself, thinking that maybe they were right. Was I going mad? I was on so many tranquillisers that sometimes I didn't even know what day of the week it was.

Then I had a breakthrough. One day, my friends Kay and Ann were sitting with me at home. They'd dropped me off after a day out but had decided to stay on a little longer for a cup of tea. The phone rang and I automatically froze. Seeing my reaction, Kay picked up the receiver and heard it for herself. The heavy breathing had begun as usual on the other end of the line. Kay gestured to Ann, who tiptoed over. The two of them shared the receiver, both listening in. At last, I had witnesses! I wasn't going insane – this was really happening.

After a while, they put down the phone.

'Oh, Jacqui,' Kay said, wrapping her arms around me, 'I can't believe that you have to put up with that after all you've been through. We need to call the police immediately and get them to take this seriously.'

Relief washed over me. It wasn't in my head after all.

Both of my friends were furious that no one had believed me. They contacted the police to tell them what had just happened. Ann spoke to an officer at the station.

'Doesn't she have enough to cope with without all of this too?' I heard Ann say, as she scolded the officer on the other end of the line. 'It's just unbelievable that you've let her think that she's somehow imagined all this.'

Moments later, there was a knock at the door. I froze in my chair, and Ann went to answer the front door. The village bobby had arrived to discuss the crank call. He explained that, to have my home phone tapped, Nottinghamshire police would have to go to the Home Office for special permission.

Thinking that nothing would be done, I became very upset and frustrated. Seeing my distress, the police officer promised to speak to the local telephone exchange in Plumtree to see if there was anything they could do. After twenty minutes, the officer left, having promised to sort something out. I thanked him for his kindness.

Later that afternoon, the telephone exchange agreed to put a special 'tap' on our home phone. 'Whoever it is that rings you, try to keep them on the phone for as long as you can,' the policeman told me.

I did this over the next few days, but soon those days turned into weeks. The caller always rang off before the call could be traced. Then, one day, about a fortnight later, the phone rang. I was home alone. I glanced at the clock on the wall in the front room – it was the usual time for the crank call.

As usual, no one spoke, but I knew that they were hanging on the other end of the line as the breathing commenced. I was worried that they would hang up too soon, so I tried to think of something, anything to say that would keep them on the line.

'I'm sorry, I can't hear you,' I began nervously. 'Please can you speak up?'

Then I panicked slightly. What if they put the phone down before the trace could be made? I had to think of a way to keep them on the line.

'Is that you, Mum?' I asked. It was a ridiculous thing to say but the first thing that popped into my head. The telephone exchange were listening in, but, when I said the word 'Mum', the operator thought that I was speaking to my mother and unplugged the tap.

After that, whoever was making those sick crank calls became wise – they never rang me again. We never did find out who it was, but I had my own ideas. I was convinced it was Colette's murderer. Was he watching the house? Did he know I was home alone and scared? Where was he hiding?

I put these fears to the police – in particular that I

thought I was being watched – but they didn't think that Colette's killer lived in the neighbourhood.

'He'll be long gone by now,' an officer insisted.

But I knew in my heart and in my head that this evil sadistic bastard was somewhere watching me. Nothing anyone said could or would convince me otherwise.

'I don't care what anyone says,' I'd say. 'Colette's murderer knows this village and he is hiding somewhere in it.' I repeated the same thing over and over again. But was I going slowly mad, imagining things that weren't there? Or was my premonition right? At the time I could not know.

As if losing a daughter wasn't enough, we endured these twisted hoax phone calls and then had strangers' cars parking right outside our home. They were journalists and press photographers. Cameras would flash as soon as we left the house, waiting to get a photo of the 'murdered girl's mum'. It was a living nightmare – no one was prepared to let us grieve.

Then came more people and more cars. This time, they were ghoul hunters – people who had nothing better to do than torment me and my family by taking in a tour of the murdered girl's home. They parked as close as they could to our home, watching and waiting for an opportunistic glimpse into our hellish world. It sickened me beyond belief. We had no privacy just when we needed it.

Three weeks after the murder, a memorial service for Colette was planned in nearby Plumtree church. To this day, I still don't know who arranged it but I believe it was suggested by the school along with the vicar of Plumtree, a man called Stephen Oliver. It was a kind gesture but I really did not want to go. I was suffering from panic attacks and found it hard to breathe as soon as I stepped over the threshold of the front door and out into this cruel world – the one that had snatched Colette from me. But I was persuaded to attend the memorial by the doctor and Tony. They felt that, as her mother, it would be the right thing for me to do. Our GP even advised me to put on my make-up and go to the church as the Jacqui that everyone knew. But how could I? What would people think? My daughter lying in the mortuary while I turn up at the church plastered with a full face of make-up. What kind of a person would people think I was?

I did as they said, but I didn't wear a scrap of make-up – the lines of grief, pain and anguish were etched in my face for all to see. As I walked into the church that cold November day, I felt all eyes turn to look at me. Did I look like the grief-stricken mother? What did people think of me? Did they blame me? Was I somehow to blame? I saw everyone but at the same time I saw no one.

Moments later, I struggled to take my next breath. The blood seemed to rush from my body and I felt dizzy. I collapsed on to the hard quarry tiles, hitting my head heavily as I went down.

I don't recall what happened next, only the concern on other people's faces as they witnessed my own personal meltdown. People ran from all over to help me. Their faces and then hands pulling and lifting me back up on to my feet. Normally, one would feel a flush of embarrassment at having fallen quite so publicly, but the medication had blunted any emotions that I once had.

Before I knew it, a car door swung open and I was eased gently into the passenger's seat. I still couldn't say who was driving, but someone took me home that day and helped me back to bed.

In December, just weeks before Christmas, the police told me that they had received a letter just seventeen days after the murder. However, up until this point, they had decided not to make it public as it was being analysed for vital clues.

'We think it's from Colette's killer,' a detective informed me.

'How do you know it's from him?' I asked.

'Because of what he's written in it.'

The officer began to explain that all the press reports had described that Colette had been naked when she was found. All her clothes had been dumped in a culvert – all except for her blouse. Only her closest family, her killer and the police knew about the white blouse that had been knotted around her wrist. It had to be him.

The letter read:

'As it is you will never find me. I was in a hut for hours waiting for a girl to return from horse riding. No one saw me.

When the car came with keys I could not help take it. Masks are common around Haloween [sic]. No one knows what I look like.

65

That is why you have not got me.

I go soon and then you will never get me.

I know I strangled her when a car past [sic]. She would have got me caught but she was not dead when I left her. Maybe the cold killed her. Cars past [sic] when we were there.

I thought she would be alright. I drove around and ended up at Keyworth.

I don't know it so I drove around to find out about the place.

I left the car there to fool you and walked back across field.

To show it was me did she wear a blouse?'

I was stunned and sickened beyond belief. The letter preyed on my mind. I thought what a dangerous and evil man Colette's killer must be. What kind of low depraved scumbag would dare write a letter like that mocking us all after what he had done? He was mocking us as a family and the police. What sort of sick gratification was he getting from this? I wept in front of the police officer.

The letter had been received at the Huntingdon Street sorting office around 3.15pm on Thursday, 17 December. It could have been posted in any post box in the City or County of Nottingham, with the exception of Worksop and Doncaster, whose mail is sorted in Doncaster, South Yorkshire.

The police explained that the contents may or may not have been written by Colette's murderer, but that there were certain aspects in it which pointed to it being from the killer.

It had been written on plain paper, possibly cartridge paper, having been cut from a larger sheet. Police experts described how it had been written with a mapping pen in a brown/red-coloured ink. They explained how the style was not a natural one. The letters had been formed drawing lines along a straight edge, such as a ruler, rather than a stencil, to give the appearance of a computer print-out. Throughout the letter, an exclamation mark had been used instead of the letter 'S', which the police said indicated that its writer had knowledge of computers. I can't quite remember why – it must have been something to do with computers as they were back then.

I truly believed that the letter had come from the killer and that he was watching and taunting us all, laughing at us from afar. I just prayed that, somehow, his disgusting boastful letter would prove to be his undoing.

I never did return to my job working for Lancôme at Debenhams. My employers had been supportive throughout my ordeal, and had kept my job open for me for the past three months. But, in my heart of hearts, I knew I wouldn't be able to go back to my old life. So, one day, I pulled out a piece of paper and began to write. I told my boss that it didn't seem fair that they were keeping my job open for me for all this time. I really couldn't say when I would be in a fit state to return to work, so felt it best that I serve my notice. That day, another little part of my 'normal' life died.

In March, five months after Colette's murder, the police arrived at my home with a form which they explained was her death certificate.

'You have to take this to the register office in Nottingham to register your daughter's death,' they told me.

A few days later, I arranged to meet my mum Joyce and we travelled to the register office in Shakespeare Street, Nottingham. I didn't want to be there, as I didn't want anyone to know who I was. I felt so exposed. We walked into a big room with a long desk running down one side with a glass front on it, opposite rows of seats where you waited to be seen.

I went up to the desk and a stern-looking woman in her late forties looked up from what she was doing and asked if she could help.

'I've come to register my daughter's death,' I told her, handing her the paper that the police had given me.

She took it from my hand and asked us to take a seat, which we did. Then she took the piece of paper and disappeared from view.

Moments later, she reappeared at the window, waving the certificate in her hand over the top of the glass partition for all to see. 'Mrs Aram, Mrs Aram,' she shouted across the room. 'This is *not* a death certificate; it's a body release form.'

I looked up at her and wanted to die right there and then. Did this woman not have any compassion in her pinched little body?

I turned to my mother. 'I can't believe this,' I said, as I felt everyone turn to look at us.

The room was packed with around 25 people, all craning their necks to look at me, having recognised my name from the newspaper and TV reports. There were a mixture of people all there to register milestones in their lives, some were happy events such as a birth or a marriage, but mine wasn't. I felt hurt and exposed. The woman behind the desk had just made a horrible experience so much harder to bear. I got up from my seat to face her.

'Stay seated for a moment or two; the registrar wants to see you,' she instructed.

Shortly afterwards, we were called into another room to see the registrar but we had to walk past a row full of people to get there. My heart was thumping as I felt every single pair of eyes on me.

We went through the door and into the registrar's office.

'Please sit down,' he said. 'Mrs Aram, this is not a death certificate, this is a body release certificate.'

'Yes,' I replied curtly, 'so I've just been told. Well, I say told, more like shouted at across the crowded waiting room outside.'

The registrar shifted uncomfortably in his seat.

'Everybody now knows who I am,' I told him. 'I came here wanting no fuss, and didn't want anyone to know who I am, but now the world and his wife knows exactly why I'm here.'

The registrar cleared his throat. 'Er, well, if you want, I can phone the coroner now and get her body released for burial,' he said. It was his attempt at making peace.

'I don't want you to do that for me. I can do that myself – I can do it through the police.'

'Yes,' he agreed, 'but you need to have her body and you need to have her buried, and I can do it for you.'

'Yes,' I told him, 'but we don't want her buried. We want her cremated.'

'But, Mrs Aram, you won't be able to have her cremated,' he told me.

'So I keep being told, but, when I do have her body for release for burial, I can do it through the police.'

'OK,' he agreed in a curt voice, 'but, as it is, you've come to the wrong office – this should have gone to the office at Bingham.'

Bingham was at the other side of the city and I didn't have the strength to travel all the way over there, so, in the end, I left it to the police to sort it out for me and register Colette's death.

My hellish day wasn't over yet. There was more in store for me on the way home.

After stopping off for a coffee to compose myself, I left my mum in the city centre and caught a bus back home to Keyworth. As I got on, I found a seat near the front, facing two long side seats which ran along the edge of the bus. It was four o'clock, and the bus was crowded. On the side seats, there was a gaggle of gossiping women on their way home from work. No one had noticed me getting on as I sat straight down, taking my seat quietly. I felt self-conscious because my picture had been in the paper, and at the same time I felt vulnerable because of what had just happened in the register office.

Suddenly, these women started talking about Colette. They were gossiping about my daughter's murder across the aisles of the bus. One woman piped up, 'Yes, well someone I know says they found her dying in a phone box.'

My God, I thought, What are these women talking about? What are they saying? I felt my heart and head begin to pound as I listened to this rubbish.

In the end, after 25 minutes of hearing this nonsense, I leaned forward and touched one of the women on the shoulder.

She turned to face me, but still didn't recognise me as Colette's grief-stricken mother.

'Excuse me,' I said, 'do you mind, that's my daughter you're talking about.'

The penny dropped and the woman was mortified when she suddenly recognised my face. She flushed bright red and turned around, away from me. 'Oh, I'm really sorry,' she mumbled back.

The other women all looked embarrassed too and they glanced down at the floor of the bus. After that, no one spoke again and we travelled the rest of the journey in complete silence.

I got off the bus after three more stops, no doubt much to the relief of the other passengers. The atmosphere had been tense and uncomfortable. We'd been almost home by the time I'd summoned up enough courage to tap the woman on the shoulder.

I felt sickened as I walked back home. All these people wanted to be in on Colette's murder, as though somehow they thrived on our misery. They want to be partly involved, but why? Was it part of human nature or was it just morbid fascination?

As soon as I walked through the front door, I burst into tears.

'Whatever's the matter?' Tony asked, concerned.

'I've just had the most awful day,' I wept as I began to explain what had just happened. I couldn't stop crying. 'I just can't believe people can treat us like this. Don't people have any feelings?'

Tony shook his head. He was as disgusted as I was.

To make matters worse, we were still getting the ghoul hunters parked outside.

'Why won't they just leave us alone?' I wailed.

Colette's funeral was held the following month. I was told that it was time she was buried so that I could come to terms with the fact that she was dead – a kind of closure.

I was not allowed to have my daughter cremated in case her killer was caught. But I was tortured with the fear that they would not let her rest in peace and that the police might order her body to be exhumed. The thought terrified me.

The doctor and the vicar told me to stick it out, to demand that my wishes be granted – that Colette be cremated. In the end, I reached a kind of stalemate with the police on the matter, so the vicar insisted that I have her buried. But first he made me a promise.

'If you have her buried and the police catch him, I

promise that I will go to the bishop himself if I have to in order to stop them from exhuming Colette's body.'

I reluctantly agreed. It was the only reason Tony and I allowed her to be buried. The vicar and my doctor were in firm agreement. This was the only way, emotionally and mentally, that I would ever come to terms with the fact that Colette was dead and never coming home

Financially, we were struggling though. I wanted Colette to be buried with dignity but I didn't have a clue how we were going to afford it. One day, the police arrived with a cheque for £2,000. To this day, I still don't know where it came from, but it was money to pay for Colette's funeral. I was adamant that my daughter would have a beautiful funeral. I insisted on a beautiful coffin made from the strongest wood they had – I wanted Colette to be protected as much as possible so she could rest in peace – and a black marble headstone with gold lettering. On top of this I had ordered extra funeral cars for all the family and close friends.

Tony wanted a fitting funeral for Colette, but he did ask me why I had to have all these very expensive things.

'Because she didn't arrive in this world a pauper and she's certainly not going out that way. She didn't deserve to die so she's not going to have a pauper's funeral. Even if I have to have a bank loan to bury her, I will.'

I couldn't believe that I had to explain myself to Tony; it was as though a conflict between us had begun.

It was just before Easter in 1984 when my family and I filed once again into Plumtree church. My daughter's funeral was kept secret from everyone as the police didn't want ghoul hunters or the press present. In short, we didn't want a circus. I was drugged up to the eyeballs; the doctor gave me some kind of special drug to get me through the day. The detectives were paranoid that news of the funeral would somehow leak out. It was hard for us all as there was so much security – including a police guard – outside the gates leading to this little church.

The local funeral directors, Lymes, had organised everything with precision. Despite the tight security and secrecy of the funeral service, Mr Lyme himself walked all the way from our house to Plumtree church, wearing his top hat and tails and carrying a silver cane in front of the family car. Only close family and friends were invited, but the church was packed.

The Godfreys were there, including Russell. I felt for Russell in particular. After Colette's body was found, he'd been taken away by the police for routine questioning about her murder. That poor boy. He was just 17 years old and terrified. We knew that he'd done nothing wrong but the police were just doing their job. They had to question everyone involved to rule them out by a process of elimination.

I was concerned about his parents. Did they think that we had asked the police to question Russell? I prayed that they didn't and that they knew us better than that. We knew he was innocent from the start. I worried how they were coping with it all. But I was more concerned about Russell. If it hadn't been for his quick thinking and telephone call to me the night Colette vanished, we wouldn't have alerted the police and carried out the search. At least he had given the police a fighting chance of finding Colette. Only they didn't find her quickly enough to save her life.

Now, in the cramped, icy cold church, Russell looked heartbroken and awkward, but I was glad he was there. He stood united among some of Colette's closest friends. It felt odd to see so many young people at a funeral. Even more surreal was that the girl lying in the coffin was my sweet 16-year-old daughter. You never expect to be burying your children. If Colette had been sick, then maybe I could have planned or prepared for something like this, but she was a perfectly happy and healthy young girl.

The police told us that, had she lived, Colette would have been severely brain damaged because of her injuries. She would have had no quality of life, they said. But how could they know for sure? At least I would still be able to hold her in my arms and to protect her from further harm.

It was a very solemn funeral service; I saw a sea of faces but took in no one in particular. Everyone looked shell-shocked. Most people were crying, while others couldn't even look at one another, let alone Colette's coffin resting at the front of the church.

I was red-eyed and crying throughout. When the tears ran dry, I became numb and shut off from everything and everyone. I didn't hear anything that was said by the vicar, Stephen Oliver, in the church. I don't remember the music and I don't recall any readings. One thing I did notice was the white flowers – I'd insisted that everyone send them, and they had. White because it represented purity and, until that bastard fouled her body, Colette was as pure as the driven snow.

We stood shivering around the graveside. I dropped a single red rose on to the top of her coffin as it was lowered into the ground. I looked around. Mum, Tony and Mark were standing near, ashen-faced. Someone began to throw soil into her grave. In a heartbeat it suddenly became too much to bear. I knew that this was my final goodbye to Colette. I felt the strength drain from me suddenly; my legs buckled and I fell to my knees on the cold, damp earth at the edge of the graveside. I remained that way. No one knew what to do. Some people were upset and had to walk away. I think I would have remained there forever but as I glanced up I saw my son's face crumpled in pain and anguish. I had to be strong for him. I composed myself and allowed others to hold me back up. This was my final goodbye.

I thought about my father's funeral just weeks before. He'd died just six months after Colette, but we buried him before her. I had never been very close to my dad, as he and my mum had divorced years earlier. But now to be burying two members of my family in such a short time was too much to bear.

When I was a child, my father had always been very strict. We had a regimented upbringing and he had a bad temper. But all of that had now been forgotten. He was my dad and I had loved him. During the latter years, Dad had tried to make amends. He did this by spending time with Mark and Colette. Now it hit me hard, knowing that he'd tried to be there for her and me but that, in the end, none of us could protect Colette when she'd needed it most.

My father had been a tall man, standing at over 6ft 2ins. On the day he died, he'd been having a shower when he suffered a massive heart attack. He fell out of the shower and landed heavily behind the bathroom door. No one was able to get through the door to rescue him. By the time the ambulance had arrived, the paramedics managed to shift the door but it was too late – my father had gone. We buried Arthur in a churchyard in Bulwell, Nottingham. His funeral was very emotional for us all.

I struggled to cope with two deaths in the family. It affected every area of my life. Now, it seemed as if the threads holding my marriage together were slowly beginning to come undone.

It is often said that grief can unite a family but, in our case, it tore us slowly apart, bit by bit. We'd been there for one another in the beginning; when the police found Colette's body, the ongoing investigation and her funeral, but the following months were harder. I wanted to talk about Colette constantly, but Tony just wanted to shut his emotions away. I thought he was being cold. Our daughter had been murdered but he wouldn't talk about her when that's all I wanted to do. I now realise that he was just dealing with things in his own way.

Mark shut himself away in his bedroom at night. He was constantly haunted by what he'd seen that day.

One day, he turned to me. 'Mum, what's happened to us? What's happened to you and Dad?' he asked.

I had no answers. The truth was I didn't know. All I knew was we'd lost our little girl and now we'd lost one another. What, indeed, had happened to us?

Colette's murder had been a hand grenade thrown into the middle of our happy family unit. We'd all been blown to smithereens by the impact and were now shards of our former selves, fragmented and broken.

And all the time the police continued their hunt for the man who had not only taken Colette's life that day, but whose brutal actions were slowly destroying us all.

CHAPTER 4

THE
INVESTIGATION

As the police investigation got going, detectives involved in the inquiry received repeated requests for interviews from newspaper journalists. I found these particularly harrowing as the last thing you want to do is to speak to a stranger about the murder of your only daughter.

I was a normal mum-of-two who had been catapulted into a huge media spotlight and I was finding it difficult to cope. To make matters worse, Tony couldn't bring himself to do press interviews. As time went on, he withdrew from everyone; there was no right or wrong in all this, it was just his way of coping. So in the end it was down to me.

Looking back, I now realise that Tony was dealing with Colette's murder in his own way but –rightly or wrongly – just when I needed his love and support, I felt totally and utterly abandoned. I was at the mercy of a press hungry for news and updates on how we were coping. I knew that this insatiable hunger must be fed so that Colette's case did not flicker and fizzle out of the news. If it did, I thought we would never stand a chance of catching the monster that had done this.

Deep down, I wanted to be left alone to grieve in private – to die quietly, even – anything to get away from this unfolding nightmare. But the opposite happened.

The nightmare intensified. Everyone wanted a little piece of me. People were coming at me from all different directions; I felt pulled and tugged at until there was nothing left for my shattered family. The pressure was unbelievable.

I was like jelly inside. I could barely function. I needed support, not to be fed like fresh meat to the hungry wolves of the media. I didn't have a single ounce of strength left inside me – there was nothing left to give. But I knew that I had to do this and do it alone. I had to force myself and summon up courage from deep down within. I needed to do this for us, but, most importantly, for Colette.

The police hunt continued. A picture had been built up of both Colette and her killer's movements on the night she was murdered.

Colette had left home at 8pm to walk to Russell's house. She saw some friends on the way and stopped to speak to them briefly – this was the last time she was seen alive. She failed to arrive at Russell's home and her naked body was found at 9am the next morning. She had been sexually assaulted and strangled.

A man was seen in West Bridgford area – only five miles away – at 4.30pm on the day she was murdered. He was hiding in hedgerow, watching girls riding horses. A rag was later discovered there by police, which contained semen; he'd been masturbating while watching those girls.

It was from here that he stole a red Fiesta. The car was seen in numerous locations throughout Keyworth and the surrounding areas. Between 6.20pm and 7.20pm the same evening, the driver was said to be stalking girls and asking repeatedly for directions. He'd attempted to abduct another girl. He'd tried to convince her to get in the car saying it was warm and dry and that he wouldn't bite, but she'd refused – it had saved her life. One witness even claimed that he had a knife; he'd seen it in the suspect's hand as he walked back to his car. The same resident was so concerned that he'd taken a note of the car registration and given it to the police.

At 8.14pm, another witness in our village heard screams and the sound of a speeding car. Police now believed that this was the moment Colette was abducted by her killer.

Within two days of Colette's murder, the landlady from the Generous Briton pub called the police. A man had been in there drinking around 9pm on the evening of the murder. The landlady noticed that he had blood on his hands; he later washed them in the gents' toilets and police were able to retrieve the paper towels from the wastepaper bin. They had all been sent off but only one contained blood – Colette's blood.

Two-and-a-half weeks after her murder, detectives received the killer's Ripper-style letter taunting them, boasting how he'd never be caught. Both the towel and the letter were now vital clues in the hunt for my daughter's killer. They had detectives working on the case around the clock. But they also needed my help.

The police were eager to keep Colette's murder appeal in the press, so they arranged for me to do an interview with the city's evening newspaper, the *Nottingham Evening Post*. It was 22 December, and we were facing our first Christmas alone without Colette. I was worried that the excitement of forthcoming festive frivolities would take over and that people would forget about her and just move on. In short, I was terrified that the case would go cold.

'I don't want to do it,' I admitted to Tony the night before the interview.

It would be the first time that I had spoken publicly about my daughter and our loss. But Tony didn't want to do it either. If I didn't, who would be there to fight her corner for her? Colette couldn't do it; she was dead and as cold as the ground where she'd been left to die. I had to do this for my daughter, to get justice for her.

The police needed me to keep Colette's name in the public spotlight, help jog memories in the hope that the next phone call could be the one to nail her killer.

With a heavy heart, I sat down at home one afternoon with a newspaper reporter from the *Evening Post*. He was a polite man but he had a job to do, so I sat back waiting for him to fire his volley of questions at me. This had now become my job and another thing to deal with. The journalist asked me how we would get through Christmas, a special time of the year for any family, but our first one without Colette.

I thought for a moment. 'The evil man who killed Colette has destroyed all our lives as well. We will not be celebrating Christmas,' I explained numbly.

The reporter wrote everything I told him in neat shorthand in a notebook perched on his lap in our tiny living room. It felt odd, alien, to be doing this, the kind of thing that you see portrayed in films or on TV. But now it was being played out in the front room of our home – our lives had become the drama that everyone was talking about.

I tried my best to convey to him the enormous hole in our lives left by Colette's brutal murder. But how could anyone even begin to comprehend such a massive personal loss? In the end, I just told the truth.

'If I am in the house on my own,' I began, 'I can't go upstairs after eight o'clock because that is the time that Colette disappeared from our lives forever.'

I felt silly admitting it but it was true.

'I can't explain it,' I said. 'I can't bear to be on my own in the house at night.'

The reporter nodded as he wrote. 'What about Colette's bedroom?' he asked gently.

'I haven't been in Colette's bedroom since it happened. I just can't go in.' I was choking back my tears.

The reporter was sympathetic and allowed me a moment to compose myself. I reached for the tissues and dabbed away my tears but nothing could hold them back now as they went into freefall, tumbling down from my face and on to my lap.

'We are all absolutely devastated by what has happened. We have only just started going out and meeting people again.'

My voice was trailing off in a whisper.

'In a strange sort of way, I feel as if I've done something wrong. It's a strange feeling, I can't explain it. It's like a nightmare.'

The journalist asked about the killer's letter to the police weeks before that had recently been made public. He wanted to know if I thought it was from Colette's killer. I told him I did. I also added that, in a roundabout way, the killer claimed he did not mean to kill Colette, but that, as far as I was concerned, it was premeditated. Suddenly I went into a rage.

'I wish there was some way I could fight to bring back capital punishment,' I shouted, unable to contain myself. 'I want the maximum penalty for this man.

'Colette was just at the stage where she was blossoming into a young woman,' I said, now a little calmer. 'She had just started work.'

I smiled as I remembered. 'She was always laughing and playing practical jokes. There was always laughter in our home. Now there is only this deathly silence.'

It was true; since Colette's death, it was as though the three of us, Tony, Mark and I, had forgotten how to communicate. It was so frustrating that Tony would not talk about Colette. For years, I held this resentment towards him inside me, but now, only years later, do I realise that it was his way of dealing with her death – a form of self-protection.

The journalist asked if I had anything to add.

'This man must be caught, not for Colette's sake but for the sake of other youngsters. He must be put away so that he cannot do this again,' I insisted.

The reporter nodded in agreement, closed his notebook, shook my hand and thanked me for my time. It had been a difficult interview, the first of many which would need to be done over the forthcoming months and years.

The following day, the newspaper ran my interview on the front page with the headline: Murder Mum's Nightmare. It read:

'There are no decorations on the walls. There is no Christmas tree, no presents. For Jacqui Aram, husband Tony and son Mark, Christmas 1983 will be a nightmare.

'For as others celebrate, the Aram family will be remembering the tragedy which destroyed their lives – the brutal murder of 16-year-old Colette.'

I wept as I read. But we had made the front page and hopefully it would make an impact on those filling their shopping trolleys in supermarkets with food and presents for Christmas. We needed that vital call – the break-through to help catch this monster. Someone out there must know who he is, I thought. Someone must suspect a brother, a son, a husband? I needed to get the public on side to catch her killer. I didn't want my daughter to be forgotten.

Days later it was Christmas. Needless to say, there were no celebrations of any kind. We were still deep in mourning for our daughter and trying to come to terms with what had happened to her.

I took my frustration out on the police.

'Why haven't you caught him?' I yelled down the phone at one of the detectives, angry tears filling my eyes. 'You won't catch him, will you? He's too clever for you. You will never catch him and I will never get any justice for my lovely Colette.'

I was lashing out verbally but the police officers were gentle. I felt like a woman possessed. I was frustrated by their lack of progress and how slowly the case was moving. The killer must have been revelling in our frustration too. He'd even written to the police mocking them from afar. He was cocky and vicious. He knew the more time that passed, the more chance he had of quite literally getting away with murder – my little girl's murder. He was cruel and heartless but he was also smart and cunning.

'Jacqui,' the detective insisted gently, 'you need to have more confidence in us. We will catch him and we won't rest until we do. This case will never be closed until that moment.'

But how was I supposed to believe them? The killer had sent a letter saying they'd never catch him. How was I meant to believe that they would?

Still, my remarks about capital punishment in my first newspaper interview caused quite a stir and soon I was front-page news again, this time in a New Year campaign to bring back hanging. My hatred for the killer knew no bounds and I wanted him caught so he could face the death penalty for imposing the same on my daughter, who had been on the brink of adulthood and the rest of her life.

The local paper ran an article headlined: Let the killer hang. Underneath I was pictured holding a photograph of my precious Colette.

'I believe that there is only one punishment fit for premeditated murder,' I told the newspaper, 'and that is death.

'Obviously, there are some categories of murder – crimes of passion – which do not carry the same degree of premeditation. But the monster that did this to my Colette does not come into that category.

'When he is caught, the best we can expect is that he will be sent to prison for a life sentence. But what does that mean? He could be out again in a matter of years and he could do the same thing to someone else.

'All the time he is in prison my husband will have to work and pay taxes to keep him there.

'I was pro-capital punishment before this happened, but obviously I am even more so now. The problem is we feel so helpless. But we are sure many more people feel like us and would be prepared to support our campaign.'

I asked people who wanted to support the campaign to write to us, adding, 'I want to do something positive to try and bring back capital punishment. We feel it is the only penalty that people like this creature that destroyed Colette deserve.'

We had hundreds of pages of A4 paper printed up and asked people to back our campaign and sign up in support. Many sent letters to us asking for copies so that they could rally around friends and neighbours and take the campaign further afield.

I expected a trickle of letters to follow the article, but what I hadn't anticipated was that they would arrive at our home in their hundreds. It was unbelievable. I received bundles of letters every day. Soon, we had thousands and thousands of signatures and addresses of the general public who identified with us and our campaign. These people were of the same mind, especially when it involved the cold-blooded killing of an innocent child. Colette had been my child but she could have been anyone's daughter. We needed a strong deterrent to stop these sexual deviants from killing our children.

Many of the letters were supportive with offers of help to collect signatures on our behalf and bring about a change in the law; a few others were less supportive.

Just after Christmas, a letter handwritten on a small piece of blue paper arrived at our home, it had been written by an older lady.

It read:

'Dear Mr and Mrs Aram, although I do not know you personally, I still feel deeply for you in your grief. However, I must also state that I think it is wrong for you to campaign for the reintroduction of the death penalty. There is no justification ever for anyone to take another's life.

No doubt you will receive many supportive letters but it seems necessary to remind you that not all agree.

May I wish you and your family peace in your hearts.

Yours Sincerely'

I was so furious about the tone of the letter. How dare someone lecture me about compassion for others? How could I find it in my heart to forgive the man who so brutally violated my daughter? I didn't give a damn about his human rights. I didn't care about the wishy-washy rights or wrongs. As her mother, I wanted him to hang for what he had done to Colette. I immediately put pen to paper.

I wrote:

'I fully agree with you that there is no justification for anyone to take another life, especially that of a 16-year-old girl who never did anyone any harm, and who was just beginning to flower into adulthood.

I am campaigning for a referendum for the return of capital punishment for premeditated murder. For a person to plan, kidnap and murder a young girl of 16, then I say this is premeditated and justifies the death penalty.

There will never be peace in my heart until the

murderer is found, but, as I understand you, murderers and rapists should not pay the death penalty.

I really think you should also campaign for a non-police state. We could then save these taxes but put all to keeping this kind of person in comfort for a few years, so that they can come out and start again.

Disgustedly,

Jacqueline Aram (Mrs).'

Soon, tears were rolling down my face. How could I feel so much anger? Why hadn't the police caught the man that had murdered my child?

Another letter arrived, it was typed in black and red ink, didn't have an address and remained unsigned, a few days later.

It read:

'Dear Mr and Mrs Aram,

Allow me to convey to your entire family my honest and sincere sympathy in your horrific and tragic loss, words are inadequate.

But, Mrs Aram, I beg of you, do not allow your grief and loss to commit you to the restoration of hanging. There must never be another Evans or Bentley, they too like your beautiful daughter cannot be restored to life, but think what their last hours on earth were like, as they waited to be murdered for a crime they did not commit.

Regarding the efforts of the police, it is due to the

enormous distrust the British people have of them (and rightly so) that so many criminals are never caught. Their record (for catching murderers) in Nottingham is abysmal. There is more I would like to say, regarding the letter in the local newspaper (*Evening Post*), but as all letters you receive will be subject to police scrutiny, I will not.'

I was furious about this one too. What sort of person would think it appropriate to send such a thing to a grieving mother? This was scrutinised by the police and put into files along with many other strangers' letters, including those who wrote to say they supported the campaign. I think they were hoping that, after his initial letter, the perpetrator might be stupid enough to write to me direct. However, this line of enquiry didn't lead anywhere.

Instead, I was contacted by a man called Derek Kennedy, who offered to help me take my campaign to our local MP, who was then Kenneth Clarke. Mr Clarke had one Saturday put aside every month where his constituents could go along and see him.

In January, along with Derek Kennedy, I did just that.

I'd voted for this man at the earlier elections but I soon lived to regret it.

We hadn't been there long when Kenneth Clarke asked me why we were there. I told him that I lived in Keyworth and that my daughter had been murdered there in October.

'Oh yes,' he replied. 'I remember the case.' Then he proceeded to tell me about a completely different murder.

I was astounded and shook my head in disbelief. 'I'm very sorry,' I said, 'but you clearly have no idea about Colette's murder.' I went on to explain that he was referring to a different person.

He was a little flustered, but then said, 'Oh, yes, well, my wife has more chance of being mugged and murdered in a multi-storey car park than your daughter.'

I was absolutely horrified. How dare he? I could barely believe what I was hearing, so I got up to leave. I'd listened to quite enough.

'But thankfully your wife is alive and well, unlike my daughter who is cold and dead.'

It was as though Colette's murder was just another government statistic. I left that day completely deflated. I'd gone to have a reasonable discussion, to get his views on capital punishment; instead, I left there feeling sickened and disgusted.

In May 1984, it was suggested to me that it would be useful if I went along to see Doris Stokes, a world-famous medium.

To be honest, I had always thought this kind of thing was a load of mumbo-jumbo, but the police informed me that sometimes the results could be quite surprising.

'These mediums can throw up all kinds of things into the equation,' an officer tried to explain. 'Mediums like this have helped the police in the past.'

'You mean that she might shed some light on what happened that night?'

He nodded. I could see that he felt awkward admitting

that they used this type of 'technology' alongside the usual hard facts and scientific research. But, if he didn't think it was a load of rubbish, then neither would I. Anything was worth a shot, so I agreed.

Doris was appearing at Nottingham's Theatre Royal but she was staying at the plush Albany Hotel in the heart of the city.

A police officer had made the appointment in advance but had told Doris nothing about me or Colette. As far as she was concerned, I was a woman off the street arriving with a gentleman, possibly my husband, for the requested sitting.

At noon on Tuesday, 8 May, a family liaison police officer called Pete Pickering and I knocked on the door of Doris's hotel suite. An elderly lady opened the door; she was short and a little plump, with greying blonde hair. The room was bright and spacious with cream walls and green velour chairs.

Doris, who was dressed in a pale-blue skirt and blouse, pulled a little jacket around her shoulders as she spoke. 'I don't know who you are or why you are here, but it's obviously very important because I'm sure that the man with you is a police officer,' she began.

Her words momentarily took Pete's breath away. She'd been told nothing about us and had no idea about me or my daughter.

'I believe you are a police officer,' she said, looking Pete directly in the eye, waiting for confirmation.

Pete gave none at that time. We wanted her to tell us things.

Doris gestured for us to sit down on two chairs, which had been placed opposite her. I stole a glance at Pete. Her initial comments had thrown us both completely. Doris sat back in her chair and looked at me. Little did I know she was already connecting to something that no one else, other than her, could see or hear.

'I get the feeling of a young person – a girl – and the age 19 years comes into it,' she said.

I thought for a moment. Mark had just celebrated his 19th birthday, although celebrations had been somewhat muted as there was little to be joyful about. But, just as I was lost in my thoughts, Doris broke the silence.

'Who's Colette?' she asked, quite out of the blue.

My heart stopped for a moment. Again I was breathless. Was there more to this than just mumbo-jumbo?

'She's my daughter, Doris,' I replied, trying to contain my emotions.

Doris threw back her head slightly and her eyes looked up to the right. She wasn't looking at anything in particular, just off into the distance.

'Colette, come in closer,' she said, as if talking to her directly.

Doris seemed to be struggling, but she continued. 'My breath's been cut off, around my throat,' she said, clutching her hand to her throat. 'I can't breathe.'

Colette had been strangled so Doris's words cut straight through my heart.

'Trees, water nearby. Happy birthday,' she said, 'Happy birthday 19 years.'

I was astonished. 'That would be Mark, her brother.

He's just had his 19th birthday,' I said, feeling a wave of hope.

But then, as quick as a heartbeat, she seemed to be making no sense.

'I get the months November, September, December,' she told us.

'November and December were the two months after the murder. The other has no significance.'

I felt my heart sink a little. After a hopeful start, this was disappointing. But Doris wasn't finished yet.

'Come in, darling,' she said again, as if speaking to Colette. 'Come a bit closer. She said she needn't have been there.'

Then, suddenly: 'I get the name Tony.'

Not Anthony but Tony, which is all anyone who knew my husband ever called him.

'That's her father,' I explained.

'He doesn't talk much about it,' she said, looking at me sadly.

I felt the warm trickle of tears sting as they rolled down my cheeks. It was true; but no one outside the family knew that.

'He doesn't talk much about it. She was his little princess,' she added, hitting the nail right on the head.

I rummaged in my bag for a tissue. The tears were coming thick and fast now, as if a dam had burst; the gate had been unlocked and opened for all the pent-up emotion to come flooding out.

Doris continued, 'She works in a place where she's serving.'

I thought of the salon where Colette had been training before her murder. She would help and serve anyone who came into the shop from the reception.

'I get the name David. David's been very good.'

I cleared my throat.

'I can only think of my half-brother David.' I also had a friend called David George.

Doris narrowed her eyes as if in deep concentration and looked away again into the distance.

'She was assaulted. She fought hard. Someone brought me a red rose – take it back to Mum. Don't worry about me, Mum.'

I dabbed at my tears, the tissue in my hand becoming a soggy papery mess on my fingertips.

'She said she spoke to someone named Michael that day. I get the name Val, Victor or something with a V. Wait a minute, it's Yvonne. She knew the person. I get the name Steven. It comes through very strongly.'

'That would be Steven – he was her old boyfriend,' I said, nodding at Pete, who was busy taking notes.

'Why did you go off with him? I knew him,' Doris said. 'I get the feeling of a churchyard nearby.'

I was puzzled by this; there was no churchyard near where Colette's body had been found. And who knew who? Some of what Doris said was very confusing.

Suddenly, Doris said, 'She didn't suffer very much. She was probably unconscious. She was moved from one place to another.'

Pete looked up at her.

'She was scrambling to get out of the car,' she continued. 'She was just dumped in this place.'

I felt sick. Colette had been abducted by car and effectively dumped. But, I wondered, could Doris have read about this somehow in the newspapers?

'Steven. Has he got a light-coloured car?'

'He had a silver one. He was a boyfriend.'

'Car and Steven. Salon...'

She stopped at the word salon. Colette had been training to become a hairdresser but, unless she'd read every local newspaper, there was no way she would have known this.

'Gone back to work,' continued Doris. 'Coming home from work. Didn't arrive home.'

That didn't make any sense. Colette went missing on her way to her boyfriend's house but it wasn't Steven she was meeting; it was Russell. She certainly wasn't on her way home.

'She'd gone to meet her boyfriend,' I said, correcting her. By now, I couldn't help myself.

But Doris continued with the flow of information not pausing for breath. 'She wouldn't have got into the car with anybody,' she insisted. 'I get the name Robert. I get Alan.'

'My cousin's boy is named Alan.'

'I get the name Susan.'

'That's his mother.'

Susan was the little girl I'd lived with when Mum and Dad divorced. She'd been a baby when I'd gone to live with her, my aunt and uncle; Susan was the sister that I'd never had.

'She says she knew him,' Doris gasped. 'He went berserk. I didn't deserve it,' she said, taking on Colette's voice.

And then: 'Did she have auburn hair?'

'No, dark,' I replied. Yet I thought of her fringe, how she'd dyed the dark on top of the blonde – it had given off an auburn tinge.

'She said auburn hair,' Doris insisted. 'I get the name Peter.'

'That's Peter there,' I said, pointing to the police officer sitting by my side. 'I don't know any other Peters.'

'I get the name Ann?'

'She is a friend of mine,' I replied, thinking of the wonderful woman who had been there for me throughout these horrific past months.

'She's let you cry on her shoulder,' Doris said accurately.

'I get Phillip. She calls him Pip.'

This took my breath away again. Colette's ex-boyfriend Phillip lived across the road from us. Everyone knew him as Phillip, but to his family and Colette he was just 'Pip'. No one would have known this.

'I get Malcolm. That's an M. M near a railway – Melvyn or something.'

I shuddered and then spoke. 'It was a Melvyn who saw the man a few minutes before Colette went missing.'

'Colette saw him – Melvyn,' said Doris. 'Was she waiting at a bus stop or near a bus stop?'

Again, this was wrong. Colette had been walking alone up Nicker Hill.

'He pulled up, said, "Where are you going?" Without thinking she got in the car.'

I shook my head in disbelief. Colette was too sensible. She'd never get in someone's car unless she knew them.

'She says "Rose". Rose has not been very well. Went to hospital. Wedding Anniversary, happy times...'

Rose was Uncle Ken's mother who had been diagnosed with Alzheimer's disease recently. We'd been to see Ken on the day of Colette's disappearance and had spent a long time discussing Rose's deteriorating health.

'She fought hard, Peter,' Doris explained, directing this towards Pete, the police officer.

'She had a chain on.'

I grabbed at the edge of the chair until my knuckles went white. Colette was wearing a gold box chain. It was plain with no pendant. No one, other than me and the police, knew about the chain; it had gone missing during her struggle with the killer – never to be seen again.

'He pulled it off,' Doris said, referring to the chain. 'He twisted it and pulled it off.'

Doris narrowed her eyes once more, deep in concentration.

'Maniac. Bite marks. I didn't deserve to die the way he killed me,' she said.

I felt sick. What bite marks? What hadn't they told me? I glanced towards Pete in horror.

Pete looked at me and began to explain. 'She had some bite marks on her body. Small bite marks from animal wildlife but we never told you.'

I felt a sick kind of relief wash over me. I thought this

depraved monster had somehow sunk his teeth into the flesh of my beautiful little girl. I felt small tears prick up again in my eyes, filling them until they spilled down my reddened cheeks. I felt so sad, so empty inside. I just wanted my lovely girl back with me and to be taken from the middle of this surreal nightmare, still unfolding before me.

'I wasn't there, Mum,' Doris replied, again taking on the voice of Colette. 'It couldn't hurt me. Melvyn saw the car. I didn't deserve it, I was a good girl.'

The words cut through my heart like a knife. That's exactly what Colette would say.

'Mum knows I couldn't go with any Tom, Dick or Harry. He lives here – someone she knew. I get a builder's yard, or building worker. They'll get him.'

'There's a builder's yard near Perkins,' I told her.

Perkins was a new restaurant that had opened and there was a builder's yard at the back of it. But until this moment it had had no significance to either me or my family. Meanwhile, Pete continued to write everything down.

Doris concentrated for a moment and then spoke: 'He left me. He just left me, just a bra on.'

This was astonishing, no one knew about the trophy bra that this sick bastard had tied around my daughter's wrist – no one except for the police and my family.

'Just left me like a load of old garbage,' added Doris.

He had. He dumped my baby at the bottom of an old hedgerow in the middle of a deserted field, as though her precious body had been a pile of rubbish to be disposed of, away from prying eyes.

'I get the name Pat, Pam or Ronnie.'

I thought of my mum's new husband. 'That's her step-grandfather,' I explained.

But Doris already knew. 'There was a divorce,' she told me correctly. 'Her real grandfather's still on this side,' she said.

'I get the name Frank. Do we know any Franks? I've got Tony again. He can't talk about it – he's a very quiet man. I'm getting this builder's yard – building trade again. I get Pip and she goes back to Steven, Andy. She met the bloke Saturday evening with her boyfriend. Disco.'

This I will never know for sure. Colette could have met this man anywhere before, even at the salon where she worked. She could have just walked past him as a random stranger on the street; we will never know for certain if he saw her before he committed this heinous crime.

She went on to describe in detail what Colette had worn that night from the cream silky blouse to the black corduroy trousers with the little fasteners, which tied at the ankle. She even mentioned a jumper of mine that Colette had borrowed without my knowing. I'd looked everywhere for it.

Doris continued, 'I get a builder's yard again. Briggs or Gregg. I get a Ken.'

'That'll be Uncle Ken,' I told her.

'She talks about this auburn hair again. She mentions the name Richardson – building trade. She says he had a mark on his left arm. I can't get it properly – a tattoo or something. She talks about a house number – it has a four – 14, 4 or 40 something. I get the name Jeffrey with a J or a G. I'm getting builders again. I get a road to do with water. It begins with a W.'

Suddenly, Pete spoke: 'Wynbreck.'

Wynbreck was the name of a road not far from our house – could it have significance?

But I thought of another road beginning with a W, one which made more sense.

'Willow Brook,' I replied.

It was where Russell's home was situated off Nicker Hill, in Keyworth, where Colette was walking the night she was abducted and murdered.

'I'm also getting Park Road or Park Avenue.'

These had no meaning to me.

'There's a common recreation ground – a field or open space, then to another place.'

I thought of Nicker Hill, where Colette had walked that night, which has fields along one side of the road.

'There's a footpath leading to the other place,' added Doris.

Suddenly Colette's voice came through once more. 'It's all right, Mum. I was unconscious. I didn't feel any pain.'

I gasped, automatically clasping my hand against my mouth. This was horrible and at the same time comforting. My head was scrambled with all the information coming from this elderly, silver-haired lady. I scolded myself for having doubted her and this process.

'Adrian … Jason. Have you got a dog?'

'Colette had one,' I replied, my voice cracking with emotion.

'Was it Suzy or something like that?' she asked, meaning a name with the same-sounding ending.

'Mitzy.'

Doris looked at me and nodded her head in confirmation. 'Colette says, "Look after Mitzy for me, Mum." I get a builder's place again. Phillip, Andy.'

'There's Andrew,' I offered. He was a good friend of Mark's; Doris even went on to guess his surname correctly.

By now Doris was exhausted and almost finished. In a way, I wanted this conversation to go on forever. In a strange kind of way, it felt like real contact with my lovely daughter. Doris had told me so much that she could never have known. I longed to speak to Colette to hold her in my arms but I couldn't. This was the closest I'd been to her since that fateful night. I could tell Doris was nearly done, but there was more.

'There are fingerprints in the car – he's very clever,' she said.

Then Colette's voice once more: 'I tried to get out, Mum – very low seat – lying back. Not front. Dragged into the back of the car.'

Finally, Doris said she had the name Julian, and Howard too. But she didn't know whether Howard was a Christian name or a surname.

With that, she looked over at me. That was it; there was no more information she could give us. Doris was an elderly lady and she looked exhausted.

The whole session had taken just under an hour, but it felt as if we'd been in that hotel room all afternoon. I felt

103

exhausted, emotional and drained. I was also very, very spooked out by the whole experience.

As we turned to leave, Pete and I shook Doris's hand and thanked her for her time. Pete packed away his notebook and headed for the door.

As we did so, Doris called out to us. 'By the way, Pete, congratulations!'

He turned to look back at Doris, his face puzzled.

She smiled. 'You've just become a grandfather!'

Pete shook his head in disbelief, but I could see that he was clearly stunned. 'No, Doris,' he replied. My heart sank. Had Doris got it so wrong? 'I'm not a grandfather – I've just become a great-grandfather!'

Doris nodded and smiled knowingly. 'What did she have?' she enquired.

'A little boy,' Pete answered, smiling warmly back at her.

'Good. Congratulations again!'

I looked at Pete in astonishment. How could she have known that? It was all so weird. I was still drugged up so I felt like I was in some kind of surreal limbo. I was living my life in a tunnel. All I could think of was the police finding this animal and bringing him to justice. But now here I was in some plush hotel, listening to what Doris Stokes, a world-famous medium off the TV, was saying. I half-believed everything because I wanted to believe what she'd told me was true. I almost needed it, just to draw some comfort from it. But, I also reasoned that there had been a few things she had said which made no sense whatsoever.

However, Doris had changed my mind about mediums that day. I was certain that she possessed some kind of gift. Nevertheless, she hadn't given me the sort of information that I wanted – clues that would help catch my daughter's killer. Naively, I'd thought somehow that I was going to come out of her hotel room knowing who had killed Colette. I thought that she'd be able to describe this man, put a name to him, but it wasn't like that. I suppose that my expectations had been too high.

Once home, I relayed the conversation to Tony, who listened intently to every single word. Until that day, Tony, like me, had thought that the whole thing had been a load of old mumbo-jumbo, but Doris had completely changed my mind. So much so that, a few days later, I asked Mum to go with me to see her at Nottingham Theatre Royal.

The theatre was packed but we weren't picked out from the crowd – there were no more messages for me that evening. To be honest, I was relieved. This was much too personal to be part of a theatre entertainment show. I wasn't ready then to share this bit of my daughter with the world; there was too much about her already in the press. I needed to preserve a little piece of Colette just for me.

Afterwards, and quite out of the blue, I received a parcel through the mail addressed to me. I still don't know to this day who it came from, but it was a book, written by Doris Stokes entitled *Voices in My Ear*. The postmark on the front of the brown envelope showed it had been posted in Nottingham. I wondered if it had come from Doris herself, but she had long since left Nottingham after the show. There was no accompanying note and no explanation, just the book. Maybe it was just a coincidence – but what a coincidence. No one, apart from my family, Doris and the police knew I'd gone to see her that day. Still, in the forthcoming months, I drew strength from the book and from what Doris had told me. Maybe there was more to the afterlife, after all.

One day, Tony and I were called to the police incident room for a general update on how the investigation was going. As we walked towards the grounds of the station, we noticed a van parked outside, a mobile cafe situated next to the local football field. There were police officers working on the beat, gathering information on the ongoing investigation and using the cafe to get hot cups of tea and coffee.

On the way into the station, we saw that they were also arranging for photographs to be taken of local men who had been pulled in to help with the inquiry. As we walked through the main doors, one of these men approached Tony.

'Don't tell me that they've pulled you in as well for a fucking picture to do with this kid that's been murdered,' he sneered.

Tony didn't know the man and he didn't know us. It was just bad timing, someone letting off a bit of steam at being called in to have his photograph taken. Indignant at having to take time off work, time out of his busy social life to help with something which meant nothing to him but everything to us.

I felt Tony's arm stiffen in anger. Then he took a deep breath and calmed down, but I wanted to smash this man's face in and Tony knew it. He quickly grabbed at my hand as I felt my fist clench.

'Leave it,' Tony whispered to me. 'Just leave it.'

The man wasn't worth it, Tony knew it and so did I, but how dare he talk about my daughter's murder like that? It was a small inconvenience for the general public to go through to get her killer off our streets. What if it had been his daughter? How would he have felt about it then?

We walked into the incident room to see the leading officer. As we entered the office, my eyes scanned across the many men sitting in it. I tried to pick out one or two but couldn't – to me they were just a monotonous blur of faces. Over 50 officers had been working on the inquiry and over 2,000 statements had already been taken.

Sitting quietly at the back of the room was Kevin Flint, a talented young police detective. I didn't know it at that time, but not only would Kevin be the man who restored my faith in the police, but he would also be the kingpin in finally bringing my daughter's killer to justice.

The briefing was both short and simple. There were leads but nothing definite. I could sense the feeling of frustration in the room.

In early 1984, months after Colette's murder, a detective came to see me with some news.

'There's a new programme that's going out called

Crimewatch UK. The same format has been running in Germany for a few years but they are going to screen it in the UK. The flagship show for it here will feature Colette's murder appeal.'

I looked at the officer. I'd never heard of such a programme and, until that time, crime had never been prominent on British TV, apart from in the odd film shown on a Saturday night. Instead, it was all fluff, chat shows and other light entertainment that filled the airwaves.

'It's already been recorded,' he informed me.

I was astonished as I didn't recall being told about it up until that moment. In the grand scheme of things, it didn't matter – anything which might catch Colette's killer was worth a shot.

But the officer shifted in his seat. He wasn't finished. 'The only thing is the reconstruction had to be recorded on the wrong side of the road because one of the householders on the correct side objected to us filming there.'

'What!' I said. 'Why?'

The officer explained that the gentleman worked in the legal profession and didn't want his property caught in a film clip to be broadcast on national television. So, instead, it had been filmed on the opposite side of the road from where she had been abducted that night, but all you could see was fields and darkness, not houses and streetlights.

I was furious. Shouldn't people be trying to help the inquiry instead of hindering it? I thought. Would it not confuse matters to show Colette on the wrong side of the road when she was abducted? Would it confuse vital witnesses and stop them from coming forward with information?

Still, the reconstruction had been done and it would be screened on BBC1 on 7 June 1984, eight months after Colette's murder.

The night it was shown, I refused to watch. Instead, when I heard the music, I went upstairs and out of earshot. I don't know whether Tony sat and watched it as we never discussed it – I didn't want anything to do with it. Mark had also refused to watch it.

It was the first case to be featured on the flagship show. I hoped it would bring someone forward. In the days following the screening, the police told me that they had had a huge response and were sifting through new information. As a result of the appeal, police received hundreds of tip-offs and were able to eliminate lots of suspects from their enquiries. However, the killer still remained at large. To make matters worse, there had also been a lot of timewasters including one woman who had called in and cried down the phone, saying she knew who'd done it. When the police looked into it, they discovered that she had been spurned and was accusing her lover of Colette's murder. It was all nonsense of course – she'd done nothing other than waste valuable police time.

There were lots of leads that were followed up, but they didn't lead to anything conclusive. Some friends told me the show had been good, but others who had watched the programme now avoided speaking to me. I don't know if it was embarrassment on their part or not knowing what to say or do. People seemed to feel uncomfortable talking about death, especially when it involved my only daughter. But this just made me feel even worse and more isolated.

It was national news now. But, even though the net had been cast far and wide, the police were no closer to catching Colette's murderer than they had been on the day he had killed her. It was becoming hard not to lose all hope that I would ever see justice done for my lovely daughter.

CHAPTER 5

THE BREAKDOWN
OF A MARRIAGE

After Colette's death, I went to see my doctor. He was a strong and dependable, no-nonsense Irishman, so he always said things exactly as they were.

'In situations such as this,' he told me, 'most marriages crack under the pressure after losing a child so suddenly. Something like this will either make or break a marriage. But 99 per cent of marriages break under the strain.'

I listened to his words and shook my head vehemently. 'I'm not worried about Tony and me,' I said confidently. 'This won't break our marriage – we're stronger than that. We're built to last. Nothing will ever break us up.'

I didn't mention the conversation to Tony when I returned home that afternoon. I didn't think it had any significance as I was certain that, as a couple, we were infallible.

But deep down in my heart I knew that something

wasn't right between us. It was as though our daughter's murder had drawn down an invisible barrier. Neither of us could see it or touch it but we both felt its presence; we knew it was there, slowly pushing a wedge between us which was growing wider with every day.

While I allowed my deep grief to wash over me for all to see, Tony kept his tucked away like a neatly pressed shirt hidden in a locked drawer. Now and again, I would see glimpses of it and he would lash out at the randomness of Colette's murder. Why our daughter? Why us? We were a good, close and happy family, so why did the killer choose to obliterate our family unit in one act of depraved wickedness?

As for Mark, we both worried about him constantly. He didn't talk about Colette much at all – he just couldn't. Every time he thought about her, all he could see was his little sister lying in the field, battered, bruised and dead, cast aside like a rag doll. If he wasn't in his room alone, he'd be out busying himself, meeting friends. Looking back, I think he found the grief at home oppressive.

All I wanted to do was talk about Colette; all Tony wanted to do was get out of the house – I felt as if he was trying to escape from me and from us. I think he felt suffocated by my grief, if you can ever feel such a thing. Instead, he returned to work as a joiner. I couldn't understand or accept it at the time but it was Tony's way of coping, by working through it.

'What can I do if I stay here?' he would say. But his reasoning fell on deaf ears because I didn't want to listen.

I wanted him home with me, not at work. To me, it felt as if he'd chosen work over me and over us. It was his way of coping but I couldn't see this at the time. I thought he was being cold. I couldn't understand it because he adored both our children, especially Colette – she was his princess, just as Doris Stokes had said. It was odd and out of character for him.

Tony wasn't a callous or hard-hearted man. In fact, he was the opposite – a total gentleman and fantastic father. But he was stifled at home and so withdrew into himself. People grieve in different ways, but Tony's way was just another nail in my already broken heart.

There were no photographs of Colette on the walls. I wanted to plaster the walls with her happy smiling image, but my husband couldn't face it – it brought back the sharp pain of our loss. He couldn't bear to be reminded.

Tony had always been the quiet type. He was shy and unassuming. It was this that initially attracted me to him. We were total opposites of one another but that's what made our marriage work. I'd always been the outgoing, bubbly one – the life and soul of the party. But now I'd assumed Tony's role. I'd become shy and withdrawn. The ongoing murder investigation had also made me fearful and paranoid. I had the constant feeling that I was being watched and didn't feel comfortable in my own home; a place that should have been my sanctuary became my prison without bars. I'd retreat into it but still I didn't feel safe. Those crank phone calls had haunted me. Was someone watching? Was it Colette's killer? Had I been the intended target, as one of the officers had suggested? But it didn't make sense – why would someone pick me or my daughter out from the crowd, with the intention of murdering one of us?

'Maybe Colette knew her killer?' an officer suggested.

I shook my head vehemently. 'I know my daughter too well. If someone had freaked her out or worried her, then she would have told me about it.'

But the police were thorough. They asked me all about Colette's movements. I recalled her work experience as a nurse at Saxondale Hospital. It had been a mixed hospital, but it also housed a psychiatric unit.

'And the school sent her on work experience there?' said an astonished officer.

'Yes, but I'm sure that the school would have done everything correctly and that Colette would never have been at any risk.'

I insisted that the work experience had nothing to do with it, but the seed of doubt had been sown in my mind. What if Colette, in her desperate bid to become a nurse, had met someone there? Maybe she'd carried out a kind act or gesture for someone but her killer, in his twisted mind, had seen it as something more? My imagination raced with the possibilities.

The police began checking out everyone that Colette had come into contact with.

I didn't know where this monster had come from but I was certain of one thing, that it was him watching me, taunting me and my family, playing with us as if we were part of some sick cat-and-mouse game.

I imagined Colette's murderer watching our house,

waiting for me to leave it. Did he know that I was there alone and scared long after Tony had left for work? Did he live in the village? Had I passed him in the street before this nightmare and smiled innocently at him in a friendly morning greeting?

The police dismissed my fears that Colette's murderer lived in Keyworth, saying that, whoever it was, he'd be long gone by now. But I had this terrible feeling that he was still here and close by, watching and waiting. Nothing anyone could say to me could convince me otherwise. I knew in my heart of hearts that this evil sadistic bastard was hiding somewhere, enjoying every moment of our misery.

'He's here somewhere, Tony,' I insisted. 'I just know he is. I think he's watching us; he's watching me.'

Tony was worried about me. To be honest, I was worried about myself, as I didn't know why I felt so strongly about this. I couldn't explain it, although everyone tried to convince me it was nonsense. I knew otherwise – a kind of sixth sense.

Things became so bad that we had a burglar alarm fitted. I also asked the police if they could fit panic alarm buttons all over our house. In the end, an ex-police officer fitted them in the hallway and at the top of the stairs, just in case we heard an intruder in the middle of the night.

But all the panic alarms in the world couldn't stop the constant dreams and nightmares. There was one particular recurring dream that would haunt me in my sleep. It was so vivid that when I awoke I would be drenched in sweat as if I was in the middle of a fever. Yet I would also be able to recount it in all its full, gory detail.

It always began with Tony and I searching for Colette, stricken with fear as we strode across a field in darkness looking for her and calling out her name. The cold would bite right through me, as it did on the night I searched for her with the police. Tony and I would desperately scour the darkness looking for an outline or blackened shape – anything like the shadow of a lost child.

Suddenly, Tony would call out. He'd seen something lying by the side of a hedge bottom in the field. As we approached, the shape would become clearer – it was Colette, but she wasn't dressed in her own clothes, instead she was naked and wearing my beloved lime-green raincoat. The very same coat I'd worn during the night search with the police. Without warning, I'd begin to scream, 'Mackintosh, Mackintosh!'

Then I would wake up. But I was never in bed.

Instead, I would be standing at the top of the stairs on the landing, drenched in sweat, scared to death by the horror vision.

My mum, who stayed with us to help me out, heard my screams and would come dashing to the bottom of the stairs still dressed in her nightclothes.

'Tony,' she would shout. 'She's done it again. My God, she's going to fall. Catch her Tony; catch her before she falls…'

Time after time, Tony would run from the bedroom, wrap his arms around me protectively and coax me back into bed. He was fantastic, he was my protector, but I could never sleep well after the first dream. It continued to haunt me as this scene was replayed in my mind like a sick film trailer time and time again.

One day, exhausted from a lack of sleep, I told the police all about my recurring dream.

Instead of dismissing me as some sort of lunatic, the officer listened intently. 'Things like this have happened in the past in similar murder cases,' he said. 'Sometimes they have brought about significant information.'

I was astonished.

'It's something we need to look into,' he added.

Soon afterwards, the police began speaking to people who lived in the surrounding villages with the surname Mackintosh.

Tony and I couldn't seem to communicate any more. Instead, he would confide in Mark. I'd hear them whispering in the kitchen together. It made me feel even more paranoid and isolated. I later discovered that they were talking about things that had come up in the police investigation – things far too upsetting for me to hear in my present state. They did it to protect me, but I'd never felt so alone in my life.

Alone and frightened, I'd sit on the chair in the hallway. It had become my favourite spot to watch and wait for Colette to return home. I'd look for her through the window but it was always someone else's daughter walking by in the street, never Colette. Still I continued to sit there and live in hope.

One day, Tony returned home from work to find me

sitting in my usual spot watching and waiting. I must have cut a pathetic and pitiful sight. Up until this point, everyone had been so kind and careful not to hurt my feelings, but Tony knew that if I was to move on I had to snap out of it – it was for my own good. He'd had enough of seeing me there night after night and it broke his heart.

'She's not coming home, Jacqui, she's gone,' he told me gently. 'Colette is dead, she's never coming home. You've got to accept it.'

But I couldn't and I wouldn't accept that I'd never see her again. I would sit there hoping that they had somehow got it wrong and that Colette would appear.

'She's not going to come home, Jacqui, she's never going to come home,' Tony insisted.

But I wouldn't believe it, not in the long months that had followed her death, not until we finally had her buried. It was only at this point that I finally accepted my little girl was never coming home. I'd needed to bury her to save my sanity.

I'd visit Colette's grave twice a week and place fresh white carnations on it. But the strange thing was that, long after I'd left the flowers behind on her grave, their pungent scent would drift along and follow me home. It would fill the hallway.

In an act of kindness, the Godfreys, Russell's family, commissioned a pastel picture of Colette while they were away in Spain. It was a lovely gesture and the picture had been taken from one of my favourite photographs of her, but there was something about it that left me on edge. We hung it in the hallway. Colette's eyes seemed to follow you wherever you stood, even if you were going up or coming down the stairs.

Then a scent of carnations began to hang heavily in the air. At first, I felt as if I was going mad. Was I just imagining it? Was my grief so overwhelming that I was beginning to imagine familiar smells linking me back to my daughter?

My mum had long since left our home following the murder, but she would still pop by to help me out with household chores. One afternoon, I had to nip out and Mum offered to do a great big pile of ironing. She decided to position herself in the hallway as it was a large space and, with me gone, the house was empty. A few hours later, I returned to find Mum still ironing, but she had moved from the hall to the kitchen.

'Why did you move?' I asked her, knowing what her answer was.

Mum didn't reply. Instead, she looked uneasy and shrugged her shoulders as if everything was fine.

'You sensed her, didn't you? In the hallway?' I said.

Mum looked up and placed the iron heavily on the end of the board. 'Yes,' she replied.

'Was it the picture?'

'I think so,' she told me, 'but I could also smell flowers – carnations.'

I knew it. I wasn't going mad!

'I just sensed that she was there with me.' Mum paused as if she was a little embarrassed to admit it. 'I was frightened, Jacqui. I can't explain it. It unnerved me, so I moved everything in here.'

It wasn't just Mum who sensed Colette. I always felt her with me in the hallway, first thing in the morning when I came downstairs and last thing at night as I walked up them to go to bed. She was still there with us. It brought me comfort.

One day, Mark and I were sitting in the lounge watching TV when he turned to me. His face was ashen white.

'Mum,' he said urgently. 'Colette's here – I can sense her.'

'I know, love,' I replied. 'So can I.'

I could smell the scent of carnations again, but there were no flowers in the house.

Other inexplicable things were happening too. One afternoon, Aunt May and my neighbour Jan were busy working in the salon. They'd given the customers cups of coffee. Once they were empty, the cups and saucers were placed on a long work surface at the side. Normally, Colette would have been there to clear, wash and put them away but they remained there for a little longer that day.

Suddenly, there was an almighty clatter of china. Jan turned her head as she heard them break against the hard floor. Both cups had inexplicably lifted themselves off the side of the work surface. They crashed down to the ground, smashing to smithereens all over the floor.

'I'm telling you, Jacqui,' Jan confessed later, 'no one was near the cups to knock them off. They just seemed to lift off all by themselves. It sounds odd, but we felt as if Colette was with us right there in the salon.'

I nodded – I understood completely.

The fact that Tony (along with most people, for that matter) hadn't believed me about the crank phone calls until my friends happened to be there to witness one had driven a further wedge into our marriage. The trust between us had been broken so everything else slowly disintegrated from that moment on.

Sexually, I couldn't bear to have Tony near me. He used to give me a peck on the cheek every night before we went to bed, but now I couldn't stand him touching me physically. All I could think was that sex was the reason my daughter had died. Colette had died for another man's depraved lust. In my mind, even sex between a man and his wife wasn't a natural and loving act any more – somehow it had become tainted by Colette's death. I simply couldn't bear it any more. As a result, the gap between Tony and me widened to the point that we were almost strangers living under the same roof. Soon, we stopped talking altogether.

We operated like robots. Eventually, I returned to work at my aunt May's salon. They'd held a position open for me for when I felt ready to return to work. I felt it was time to go back. I only worked a couple of days a week but it was good for me to escape from the house, my failing marriage and my negative thoughts.

I was worried that clients would ask me about Colette but no one ever did. I didn't cut hair at the salon. Instead, I took up Colette's old position and covered the reception so my conversations with people were purposely kept short and brief. I would smile and make appointments and show them through, but I wouldn't stand discussing my life with them. It was too painful. Often, the police would pop into the salon to see me, but I would take them into the staff room out the back. Clients would see us, but no one ever asked what was going on – I think they knew better than to pry.

Working in the salon, I still had the sense that I was being watched all the time. It was an awful feeling. I felt so vulnerable – as if I was living in a goldfish bowl. Nothing seemed to make an awful lot of sense any more. One afternoon – in an event I would not find out about for many years to come – one of the young hairdressers was stopped outside the salon by a man. He asked her things about the people who worked inside, including our names. The girl was busy on her lunch break and had nipped over the road to a nearby shop. Her mind was occupied with grabbing her lunch so she thought nothing of the conversation. But, years later; she wondered whether it had been Colette's killer, trying to ascertain if I was back there. We will never know now, but perhaps I was right that someone was watching me from the shadows.

Even though I'd smile and greet clients from behind the salon reception, my smile was thin, tight and painted on. It was a false smile. I felt on show. How was I supposed to be? How was I supposed to act? Was I playing a convincing part of the grieving mother or, by going back to work, did I somehow appear uncaring and hard-hearted?

The police informed me that they had enlisted the help of special constables to aid in the murder inquiry. Soon, reports of conversations at various homes had filtered back to me through friends and clients and those working in the hairdressers.

One day, a young special constable had been to a house which belonged to a friend of a friend of mine.

'What about Jacqui Aram, eh?' he'd said to her. 'She's supposed to be a bit of a girl, ain't she?'

I was mortified when I heard this. Was he trying to say I was some sort of loose woman? Wasn't I suffering enough, without nasty unfounded comments like this? Maybe they were saying these things to provoke a reaction from the people they were speaking to – perhaps it was part of a bigger plan. But what reaction would a comment like that provoke? It only served to sully my good name and make me feel even more vulnerable.

I didn't lodge an official complaint but instead mentioned it to my family liaison officer Pete Pickering.

'Why would he say such a thing, Pete?' I asked. 'What have I ever done for someone to say something like that about me?'

Pete looked at me apologetically and shook his head. He couldn't believe it either. The police had been fantastic. This was only one bad apple. But it had hurt me deeply.

'I've lived for my kids and my husband. I've worked hard all my life. Sure, I've enjoyed the odd weekend out with my husband or we've gone out as a family, but what have I done to deserve this?'

'I shouldn't read too much into it, Jacqui,' Pete

explained. 'They've drafted in a lot of specials for the door-to-door enquiries.'

Some days, things became so bad that I would suffer panic attacks where I could barely leave the house. It was as if every breath was being drained from me by an invisible force. Other days I wanted to run round and scream like a lunatic at the injustice of it all – I just wanted my family back. I felt bereft, like I'd lost everything. I wanted Colette here in my arms, and for Tony and me to be as happy as we were before all of this. The sad thing was that I knew deep down it would never happen. Instead, things were slowly getting worse. Tony and I would kiss each other goodbye when we left for work but we were just going through the motions – our marriage had become a sham. We were merely keeping up appearances. Financially, things became difficult for us after Colette's death. In short, we were struggling in more ways than one.

Everything was sliding away from me, my relationship with my husband and even with my son, but I didn't know what to do or how to stop it. Life was out of my control and I felt utterly powerless.

The years passed and Tony and I continued to operate within our own little worlds. I was back at work and functioning but not feeling anything in particular. I managed to pull myself together enough to arrange a party for Mark's 21st. I wanted it to be a special time for him. We'd spent the past two years grieving for Colette and sometimes I felt as if Mark had been forgotten. It wasn't intentional; with the ongoing police investigation, it was just so exhausting and hard to manage to put time aside for our home life and all that it entailed.

Up until now, I'd put all my energies into trying to help the police catch Colette's killer. But we had nothing. No new leads. It was as though the whole investigation had ground to a halt.

Now it was Mark's time. We booked the local church hall and invited 250 people to the party. It was a tall order but I insisted on catering for everyone and doing all the table decorations. We also paid to have a bar in there, organised through the local pub. It was a thank you to everyone who had supported us through this dark time in our lives. We invited everyone: Mark's friends, Colette's friends, family and even the police officers involved in the investigation.

It felt strange to hold a celebration, but I had to think about Mark. He'd been through as much as, if not more than, the rest of us, as he'd seen Colette's body lying in the field that day. I think that, to a certain degree, Mark had felt neglected and somewhat pushed out. This wasn't intentional on my part and I was the last thing I wanted. It had just happened. I loved my son dearly but felt that everything had been against him, so I really wanted to give him a big party – a huge celebration for his 21st.

It was a busy night. The hall was packed and Mark was having a great time. Some of his friends arrived and, unbeknown to us, they had practised a routine from the TV – a strip dance where the men had concealed themselves using balloons. But, instead of balloons, Mark's friends were using paper plates to hide their manhood.

'Oh my God, they've taken their clothes off!' I screamed in disbelief from the back of the hall.

Soon we all began to dissolve into laughter. My mum looked back at me in astonishment and then back at the stage full of now naked cavorting male dancers.

'Well, at least our Mark's not up there!' she tutted disapprovingly. Her disgust at the unfolding strip show made me laugh even more.

It was hilarious to watch and for a moment I quite forgot myself. For the first time in years, I began to laugh until joyful tears poured down my cheeks. It was good to feel this way once more.

My brother Michael had come up from Bristol with my nephews and nieces. In the aftermath and during the midst of Colette's murder, his eldest son Neil had been diagnosed with spinal cancer. He was only 12, and he had been in the middle of his treatment. He had lost his hair and was wearing a baseball cap. It was good to see the family, Neil in particular. For the first time in two years, he looked so well and was almost fighting fit again. That time was the turning point for Neil. He'd been diagnosed with cancer just a month after Colette had been murdered, so it had been a long and arduous journey for all the family.

We'd visited Neil in hospital down in Bristol. At that time, he had been undergoing lumbar punctures and tests, so to see him so well standing at Mark's party felt so positive. At least there had been one survivor from these dark times. Neil was living proof that life went on. Although I was still grieving for my Colette, there was a glimmer of hope burning bright in his life. He was and still is a true survivor.

It was so good to see my son having such a good time and enjoying himself with his friends. Little did I know what was around the corner.

Shortly afterwards, just weeks later, I returned home from work one day to find Mark missing. He was nowhere to be seen and neither was Zara, his old English sheepdog.

I turned to Tony, who was standing in the kitchen. 'Where's the dog?' I asked him.

'She's gone,' Tony replied.

'Gone where?'

'She's gone with Mark,' Tony said, barely able to look me in the eye.

'Gone with Mark where?' I said, as if we were playing some pathetic guessing game. 'Have they gone for a walk?'

'No,' Tony said, 'they've gone.'

I shook my head in disbelief. 'What do you mean?'

Tony looked up at me, this time he stared me directly in the eye. 'They've moved out,' he said loudly, as if to press home the point.

I shook my head. I didn't want to hear this. 'Where have they gone?' I gasped.

'They've gone to live at my dad's house.'

I was confused. 'But why would they do that? Why didn't you tell me? You must have known he was going.'

Then I recalled all the recent whispered conversations between them in the kitchen and suddenly everything made sense. I was getting angry now, and raised my voice. 'Why didn't you tell me, Tony?'

'Why should I have?'

'Because he's my son too. Why couldn't you tell me?'

'Like I said, why should I? Anyway, you seem to have forgotten you have a son.'

His words cut right through me like a knife. How could my husband know about this and not tell me? Things were worse than I thought.

'OK,' I sighed. 'I'll tell you what; if this is how it's going to be, then I think it's best if we call it a day.'

Tony looked at me.

'I want a divorce,' I said finally, the words nearly catching in my throat.

Everything had contributed to this pivotal moment; the ongoing investigation, the police leads that led nowhere, Mark moving out, being forced to exist solely in each other's company for the first time in 21 years. It all had an effect. No one was to blame.

The doctor had been right. Most marriages crumble under this kind of strain and ours had. I'd always thought I had such a strong, robust marriage, one that could survive almost anything. But it couldn't survive the fallout from our daughter's murder. We couldn't get through it together. Instead, we drifted further and further apart until there was no point in even trying to fight it any more. The deep love had been replaced by petty misgivings and misunderstandings. With no one else to blame, we had directed our anger and frustration at one another. We'd slowly destroyed ourselves and the love that we'd once held for one another. It had died and been buried along with Colette.

Tony and I agreed to separate. Still, we agreed to live together until the house was sold. I continued to do all the cooking, cleaning and washing. We lived like this for five months. It was as though I acted out my part as the dutiful wife, but we were in the midst of a divorce. My solicitor was horrified that I was still doing domestic chores for Tony. Since we were still living under the same roof, I didn't really see what choice I had. It was a very difficult time.

Once Mark had gone, there was little point in our staying together anyway. He had been the glue in our relationship following Colette's death. But, with our son away, there was nothing holding us together any more. If he'd still been at home, I truly believe that Tony and I would have stayed together. And, if Colette hadn't been murdered, perhaps we'd still be happily married today. Who knows?

It all put a strain on my entire life, so much so that I began to suffer other recurring nightmares. They felt so real that I was certain that, if I reached out, I would be able to touch them. One nightmare replaced another.

My latest dream featured a carnival parade of clowns with smiles as false as the greasepaint used to daub them on. They looked happy but in a twisted way. The atmosphere was buoyant as the carnival wound down one of Nottingham's busiest main roads. The crowd was cheering and clapping along to the music, but I felt isolated and alone – I was stuck at the back unable to see what was passing in the centre.

Men dressed in finery marched alongside the dancing parade. They called through heavy black megaphones to jolly up the swelling crowd. I pushed my way to the front between the packed lines of people so I could see what everyone was looking at. I felt the breath catch in my throat as I spotted it – a brightly coloured coffin, painted all the colours of the rainbow, was nestled right in the centre. I wondered why they would choose to have a celebration alongside a coffin, a death. The coffin was small and wooden, just like Colette's had been, and it was smothered in flowers. Roses and carnations were strewn on top in a huge pile; their strong, familiar scent filled the air and my nostrils. The aroma was overpowering. Suddenly, the performers began to shout as they clapped and danced alongside the coffin.

'She was too young to die,' they jeered in unison.

The men with the megaphones faced me and I felt all eyes turn towards me as they continued: 'Yes, she was too young to die; it should have been your turn!'

The whole crowd looked over at me and began to laugh, holler and clap as the men pointed at me with accusing fingers: 'She's to blame,' they yelled, louder and louder.

Memories of our
angel. Colette at
school, bright smile
beaming and eyes
sparkling.

Colette with Mark. The pair were our pride and joy and cared for each other deeply.

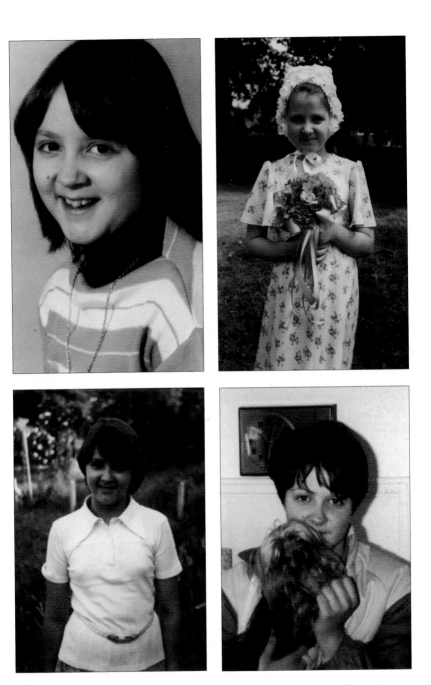

Innocence through the years. These treasured pictures are all we have left of our beloved Colette.

How I will always remember her. Joyful and kind – that was my precious daughter.

A wall of voices joined in shouting the same thing; soon their words rose above the music and the noise of the carnival. 'She's to blame, she's to blame.' Everyone sang it over and over again like a sick choir.

At this point I'd wake up, soaked in sweat. The dreams always seemed so real; I never realised it was just a nightmare until that moment of waking. I soon learned that, during times of crisis and severe stress, the mind can play wicked tricks, and mine was regularly doing just that. I was exhausted with guilt, stress and lack of sleep. In short, almost two years later, I was still blaming myself – punishing myself for Colette's murder. I felt as if I was going slowly mad. I needed a fresh start away from the chaos that had become my life.

With the family home up for sale, I put in an offer on a lovely little Georgian townhouse in Arnold, Nottingham. I was delighted when my offer was accepted, and I'd received my settlement from the sale of our old house. I took quite a bit of furniture from the house because Tony had bought a mobile home in Tollerton, a village outside Nottingham, which was already furnished. I had to move in with my mum for the first six weeks until the sale was complete. Once it was, I bought new carpets and a three-piece suite for my new home.

But Mum couldn't understand why I was going to such expense. 'Why are you buying all this?' she asked me one day.

'It needs to be as I want it. Once I'm in there and living on my own, I'll probably never be able to afford to do it again, so I might as well do it properly and get it right from the start.'

I felt torn leaving the old family home. We'd lived there for over ten years and had moved into it when Colette had been just eight years old. Tony and I had bought the house from the builder, who had built two properties. We lived in one and Jan, the manageress from the salon, lived in the other. It had felt like we were surrounded by family. I hated moving out because somehow it felt as if I was leaving Colette behind, all on her own. The constant smell of carnations in the hallway and my meeting with Doris Stokes had convinced me Colette was there. Even so, I also knew that for my sanity I couldn't go on with things the way they were. In the end, I told myself that Colette would have understood.

But it didn't make clearing out her old bedroom any easier. I gave my mum her bed for her spare room. I'd already given all her clothes away to charity but I kept all of the dancing medals and diplomas that she'd proudly won, one after the other. Along with her trinkets and some of her favourite childhood fluffy toys, Colette's personal things stayed with me for safe keeping. They remain so to this day.

It was May 1985, and I'd been living at my lovely new home for just a few weeks. By this time, I'd returned to Debenhams to work for the French skincare company Guerlain, and I was trying to rebuild my life as it had been when I was happy.

I'd had an answer machine fitted to the home phone as

a precaution to field my calls as I'd had a few silent phone calls when I'd been on my own alone at night. When I came home from work this particular evening at 6.30pm, the phone line was open and I knew someone was there on the other end of the line but no one spoke. The red light on top of the answer machine was also bleeping to say there were two or three messages waiting to be heard but, when I switched it on, there was nobody there.

Oh, God, I thought, not again.

The phone calls lasted a couple of minutes each before the caller would hang up and dial again to do exactly the same thing. It was nothing like back in Keyworth where the crank calls were constant. But it was frightening to think that someone had traced me to my new house and got hold of my private telephone number to stalk me all over again. The phone calls lasted for a couple of months but I didn't report it to the police as I thought they would think I was being paranoid. I was concerned that they would form a false opinion of me and that, when I needed them to take me seriously, they would not. So instead, I suffered in silence.

I also got the same old feeling that someone was watching the house. The property was secured by a big fence which ran all the way around the back. But I still didn't feel safe.

I confided in Mum. I felt really unnerved – other than close friends and family, no one really knew where I had moved to. How had a stranger found me? It crossed my mind that someone could have followed me home from work.

The feeling of being watched lasted the whole time I lived at that house. But who was it? Was it Colette's killer watching for clues about where the inquiry was at? Or was he just biding his time, waiting for the case to go cold and for me to go slowly insane with grief?

CHAPTER 6

THE CASE GOES COLD

The investigation rumbled on. The police continued to follow – and exhaust – all major leads but, with the arrival of the 1984 miners' strike, Colette's case seemed to fizzle out.

Valuable resources were needed elsewhere, as regular police officers had to keep public order as Britain began to erupt with one of the longest and most bitter strikes this country has ever seen. Soon the headlines were full of striking miners, wives on picket lines and families left without a vital income. People were going hungry.

The papers were full of the latest news from Nottingham and Yorkshire, and soon my worst fears were confirmed: the ongoing murder inquiry wasn't making the front pages any more. It seemed as though everyone had forgotten about my daughter. They hadn't of course; there was still a team of dedicated detectives working round the clock trying to solve Colette's murder. But the strike had a big impact on resources and finances and this affected funds. As a result, the inquiry was downsized 18 months or so after Colette's murder.

As with all murder inquiries, the case is never cold. But the striking miners and their families had knocked Colette's face and murder appeal clean off the front pages of the papers and from the top of the news bulletins. To me, it appeared as though Colette's killer had slipped through the net. He had got away with murder. We still had a big gaping hole in our lives. Everyone else had simply moved on, but how could we?

By then, my brother Michael had qualified as a police officer and moved down south with his wife and children. Yet the shortage of officers was so critical that he was drafted hundreds of miles back up to his native Nottinghamshire to man the picket lines and stop trouble and violence flaring up in the small mining communities which peppered the county.

Michael told me he'd been drafted to Ollerton. I could hardly believe it. Ollerton was just a stone's throw from where I was living. I thought – from a selfish point of view – how nice it would be to have my younger but strong and dependable brother so close. I knew he would offer me support; I was four years older than Michael but he was a tower of strength to me in the early days and continued to be throughout the rest of my life.

Even though I was happy that Michael was close by, drafting officers from police forces all over the country cost a fortune. Money that could have been put to good use paying for police overtime to help catch Colette's killer was being haemorrhaged to bring order to the picket lines. Not that I blamed the miners. I had every sympathy towards them and their cause – fighting for their own kind of justice – just a different kind of justice to mine. I saw the strike from both sides.

Was Colette's case going to be left forgotten forever? Would this mean, as her killer had so callously boasted in his Ripper-style letter, that they would never catch him? Would this sadistic evil monster be free to roam the streets and possibly kill again because the police had had their attention diverted to a national strike? Would Colette's killer be sitting in his lair silently laughing at us all, safe in the knowledge that he'd got away with murder?

I thought about it all the time. The police came to visit regularly, but each time they seemed to have less and less to tell me.

'He's going to get away with this, isn't he?' I asked, my face filled with anguish. I looked the detective square in the eye.

He shifted uneasily in his chair in my front room. Colette's face stared at him from photographs mounted in frames on the mantelpiece – a constant reminder of the young life that had been snuffed out by a single act of evil.

'We are pursuing all lines of enquiry and will continue to do so, Jacqui,' he said, trying to reassure me. It wasn't working. Far from it.

He continued, 'We will never give up looking for the man who did this to your daughter, however long it takes.' He turned his gaze from mine to a picture of Colette.

I wanted to believe him. I wanted to believe what he was telling me, but, every time I turned on the TV, the news told me that all available officers were policing the miners and the ever-growing strike.

The phone stopped ringing and the journalists stopped knocking at the door for quotes. It appeared most of them, like the police, were tied up one way or another with the same strike.

In the meantime, my family and I sat and waited.

'I wish they'd catch the bastard,' I sobbed to Mum one evening. I was exasperated. 'How long is this going to take?'

But Mum had no answers. Nobody did.

My father had died before Colette's killer had been brought to justice; then when my stepfather Ron passed away, I thought how another life had been lost without knowing who had been responsible for taking Colette away from us. There was so much pain.

Things were not good with my job back at the salon, either. It's never a good idea to work with family, especially when your family is going through an ordeal as horrific as murder. My emotions were running far too high. My aunt had bought the salon for Colette and me, but my precious daughter never even got the chance to work alongside me. The dream had evaporated and died the same day her broken and battered body had been found in that field.

The salon had been named Jacqui's – after me – but the

constant reminder that this had all been for Colette was too much to bear. My beloved aunt and I eventually had an argument about the way the salon was being run and I left that same day. We didn't speak for a year, which broke my heart as we'd always been so close. They sold the salon to another member of staff, so I decided to return to my old job at Guerlain.

My aunt and I eventually made up. She died just over a decade later, followed just two years on by my lovely uncle Ken. Like the others before them, they had died not knowing who had killed our lovely Colette.

As time went on, I became more and more frustrated.

'I wish I knew where to find the bastard,' I'd rage to friends and anyone else who would listen. 'I wish I could get my hands on him, I'd lay out my own justice on him...'

Pent-up anger, hurt and frustration boiled inside me like lava in a volcano. It changed me as a person; I suspected everyone and became suspicious of close friends and particularly men in general.

But looking for her killer was like looking for a needle in a haystack. Where could I start? If the police had no new leads, how would I, an untrained mum-of-two, know where to start looking?

The only solid thing I had to go on was a photofit of Colette's killer. It had been posted in the local paper at the beginning of the manhunt and showed two faces – one bearded, one with just a moustache. Statements taken from independent witnesses had convinced the police that they were one and the same man and detectives were certain that the beard was false.

I held the image of that photofit in my head and, whenever I was out shopping or working behind the counter, I'd scan the crowds of people passing through. The man was described as aged 30 to 35 years old, 5ft 7ins to 5ft 10ins tall, with dark bubble-curled hair, as was the fashion at that time.

I'd dream of the call from the police saying that they had caught him. I'd sit and wait for the telephone to ring but the call never came. I constantly dreamed of my day in court with me facing him – my daughter's depraved killer. I imagined him getting the maximum life sentence for his crime and the judge telling him how he'd never see daylight again.

In my heart – and against some public opinion – I wanted him to hang. I wanted to watch the life drain from him just as he'd done with Colette. He'd cut off the life inside her the night he strangled her; he'd squeezed until she fought for her last breath. Her final memory of this life would be the vicious face of her killer kneeling angry and demented as he hovered over her. I wanted him to suffer too.

But I also worried. What if they caught the wrong man? The last thing I wanted was for an innocent life to be affected by his vile crime.

I vowed to myself that, if they caught him and he didn't get a long sentence, I'd be there in my car, waiting for him to come through those prison doors. I'd wait to mete out my own justice on behalf of Colette. I dreamed of it often: the engine running, my foot on the accelerator, pressing down, revving the engine, watching and waiting to see the fear in his eyes; the same fear my daughter would have had. Watching him flee, scared for his life as I hunt him down like the animal he is.

I convinced myself that, if he was caught, he would be out of prison within ten years. I had seen it time and time again on the news. The grieving families forgotten, banished to a memory – a flashback image of grief-stricken people weeping on the court steps, while, back in the studio, the newsreader announces that the killer has been released after serving a paltry sentence. I didn't want to be like those families.

Instead, I told everyone about my plan with the car, even the police. I'd given myself away but I didn't care – I would have taken his life, just as he had taken my daughter's life and my reason for living away from me. I would have killed him; I would have done it for Colette.

I remember when Eric Morecambe died, and a friend became quite upset upon hearing the news. 'Don't you think it's sad that he's died?' she asked.

'Yes, it's very sad,' I replied, a little sharply. 'But you know what? At least he had a good and full life. At least he died from natural causes, which is more than we can say for my daughter.'

The woman looked up at me and then quickly away as if she wanted to hook her words on to a fishing line and reel them right back in again. I felt embarrassed too by my outburst. It wasn't her fault. But what had I become? This wasn't me, this wasn't the fun-loving Jacqui that everyone knew and loved. I had become an angry and bitter parody of that woman. That Jacqui had long gone and been replaced by someone frightened of her own shadow; sad, lonely, angry and carrying the deepest wound in her heart. My wound was invisible but I knew it was there, I lived with it every day – a huge gaping hole in my heart, wider than a canyon and deeper than a well.

I had become damaged goods.

My friends were a great source of support throughout this time as we waited for something, anything, to come from the police working on the murder inquiry. They knew the real me, not the bitter one. They protected and cared for me. Many would just drop by for a cuppa and a chat; others would call and insist on taking me out. At one point, a few of them got together to plan a birthday treat for me at one of my favourite places – The Victoria Club, a members-only club where you could lunch or have dinner. The place was smart, with a Victorian theme from the clothes of the waiting staff to the décor. We were all members there and with good reason.

The club was plush inside and boasted its own chauffeurs who would take our keys and park our cars around the back. I liked this because it made me feel safe. I'd spent years feeling so vulnerable, but going out on evenings like this was like having a warm comfort blanket wrapped around me – further protection from the nagging feeling that I was constantly being watched.

Many times, especially when I was still in Keyworth, I would have to force myself to go outside, even if it was just to the local shop for a pint of milk or loaf of bread. I'd often see women, old friends of mine, approaching, who, upon spotting me, would quickly glance down towards the pavement, not looking up. I knew why they did it – a fear of not knowing what to say or do, a fear that I might start crying. I knew why they avoided me, but never understood it. Just a good morning or a 'hello, Jacqui' would have sufficed, anything to stop me feeling so isolated within my own grief. But they put their own feelings in front of mine and I could never forgive them for that. Just when I needed support, I was cast aside like some kind of social leper.

When I moved to my Georgian townhouse in a new area, no one knew me as they had at the old house. I was free to come and go as I pleased. This was my new life; this is what would give me independence. I didn't tell my neighbours who I was but they must have guessed. My face had been all over the local press in the years following Colette's murder; surely one of them would perhaps recall seeing it in this context? If they did, they certainly never spoke to me about it, which made me feel better. It was as if I was somehow protected by a cloak of anonymity.

The only exceptions were my immediate neighbours – a barrister and a man who lived directly opposite me. Somewhat ironically he was called Tony. He had had a girlfriend in my old village of Keyworth. They'd been going out for quite some time but had recently split. Tony and I became good friends and, because we were both on our own, we started to socialise together. The relationship was strictly platonic but it didn't stop the tongues from wagging. If I was going for a night out with friends, Tony would come along; likewise, if he was cooking a nice meal for tea, I would get a call and an invite over to his.

I worked in town but didn't want to take my car in every day because of the extortionate cost of city-centre parking, so I'd catch the bus. One day, Tony saw me walking to the bus stop. 'Here, Jacqui,' he called as he pulled the car up alongside me. 'Hop in; I'll give you a lift.'

Tony's car was a black Porsche. It was pretty flash. Tony had his own parking facility in the city centre so after that he started giving me a lift to work. The girls at Debenhams had convinced themselves that Tony was my new rich boyfriend – my toy boy! But he was just a kind neighbour and one of the few men that I trusted.

'We're just friends,' I tried to explain one morning at work, much to the amusement of my colleagues.

'Yeah, sure, Jacqui,' one winked back at me, grinning.

Try as I might, there was no convincing them otherwise.

On Sundays, I would go and visit my friend Gina for lunch. Sometimes she would come to me; it was an unspoken agreement – something to keep me company on the long weekends as I waited for the call that never came.

My friend Val had a lifelong friend who lived out in America. Her friend had bought a cottage in a village called Woolsthorpe where the counties of Lincolnshire, Leicestershire and Nottinghamshire meet amid rolling green hills in a picture-postcard setting. It was a truly beautiful area. The cottage was called Rosy Row and it was as pretty as its name suggested. It had once been part of the tithe cottages belonging to the Duke of Rutland, and Val was the cottage caretaker. This meant we got to enjoy many sunny and happy weekends there. I'd load my car up with food and wine and we'd set off. We enjoyed long walks along the edge of the Belvoir Castle Estate, mounted high upon a hilltop in rural Leicestershire.

There was a little pub opposite the cottage where we'd go for a drink on the Saturday night before nipping back home to cook our evening meal. Despite Colette's death, I still enjoyed cooking; it kept me sane on the many long evenings that I spent on my own.

When I was busy with friends, I wouldn't have time to think about my situation – how my life was on hold waiting for a development or breakthrough in the case. It was only once I was alone with my thoughts that reality would kick back in like a solid right hook to the side of my head. It would leave me reeling. I was alone and lonely. I mourned my old, familiar life. I just wanted my husband and children to surround me once more. I didn't choose this new, cold, independent life. I wanted things to be as they were before, but how could they ever be like that again?

The police continued to visit, but due to a lack of new information these visits slowly petered out.

'That's it. He's got away with it,' I told friends.

They tried to reassure me but what could anyone say? Four years had passed and nothing.

I felt totally helpless, so I decided to do something positive, something to help others and stop my grief and frustration from swamping me entirely. I became a voluntary worker for Victim Support. It was my way of helping other people who had suffered as I was suffering myself. I was given my own ID card with a picture of me smiling out from it. The smile was false, of course. I had nothing to smile about, but at least now, for the first time in years, I had a purpose to my life. I decided to grab it with both hands.

Soon, I spent all my free time on this fulfilling and rewarding work. I would be given the details of the person I needed to visit and I always telephoned beforehand to arrange a meeting. I loved giving support to those who needed it. It was something that had not been available to us back in 1983 – the year of Colette's murder. Victim Support was a new scheme and it was working, really making a difference to those who needed it. I felt like I was giving something back to society. I was able to help others by sharing some of my own grief and, in turn, that compassion for other human beings began to heal me. The thought that I'd made even the slightest difference to someone's life helped me enormously. Slowly at first – but surely – I was beginning to heal.

I stayed in my little Georgian townhouse for two years before I was offered the chance of seasonal work abroad in Greece in 1988.

I'd been on holiday the previous year and really enjoyed myself. Then I was offered a job as a holiday rep for the following summer with a Cypriot-based company called Grecian Holidays.

I was torn about what to do for the best. Would I be

running away? I supposed I would be, but at least out there I would not be Colette Aram, the murdered girl's mum. I could be me – nobody knew who I was and no one would ever have to know anything about my past. I could be Jacqui Aram or Jacqui whoever. I could be whatever I wanted to be. This could be my fresh start, if I wanted it to be.

It felt like it might be a lifeline.

In the end, it was Mark who helped make the decision for me. 'Mum,' he sighed one day, 'it's time for you to take the bull by the horns and go and live your life. You've spent so long being unhappy and looking over your shoulder all the time. Maybe you should just do this and see where it takes you. If it doesn't work out, you can always come home. If it does work out, then all the better.'

I knew he was right. I needed to take a chance on life. With Colette and my marriage gone, what did I have to lose? I listened to what Mark had to say, and I also knew that, wherever she was, this is what Colette would have wanted – for me to be happy.

This was a potential new chapter of my life, and it was there for the taking.

I decided to take it.

CHAPTER 7

A NEW LIFE
IN GREECE

The crank phone calls and the feeling I was being watched continued right up until the day I left for Greece. I'd moved into my new home in 1985, and my divorce from Tony had finally come through at the end of that same year. Three years later, after trying to move on with my life in Nottingham, I finally admitted defeat. I couldn't escape my fears and grief; I needed a fresh start so I decided to go for it and moved to Greece to work during the spring of 1988.

Still, I wasn't sure whether to sell my house or rent it out. A friend suggested that I sell; I didn't need the stress of being a landlord and not knowing if the rent would be paid on time, he reasoned.

I considered this. My friend had a point. But, at the same time, I worried that selling my home would mean that I was cutting my ties with England and with my daughter. In the end, I decided to sell and be done with it – Colette would always be in my heart, no matter where I lived.

I never doubted for a second that I would be happy living in Greece. It was such a beautiful country. I'd absolutely loved it when I'd been on holiday there the year before. A friend had wanted to go back and work there, so we had both applied to be holiday reps for Grecian Holidays. Unfortunately, I got a job and she didn't, even though it was at her suggestion. I felt terribly guilty, almost as if I'd stolen it from her. But I had a sales background and so it helped secure the job for me. However, my friend never really spoke to me again after that, apart from a brisk 'hello'. It hurt me no end. We'd been through such a lot together but this was another friendship lost.

Soon I was jetting off to a new life on Zakynthos, one of the Ionian islands. The temperature and way of life was so different to working in a department store back in cold and rainy Nottingham. At first I felt a bit lost, but within a few weeks I relished my new role working as a holiday rep and making other people happy. I stayed for six months and absolutely loved it. I wasn't 'the murdered girl's mum'; I was just Jacqui and I could be happy once more.

Once the summer season had finished, I packed my bags and came back home to Nottingham where I settled at Mum's house for the winter months. Then I went back to Greece again. In the beginning, I'd come back at the summer season's end. But I found that the English cold and October – Halloween month – carried with it too many bad memories. After that, I decided that I would only return to England before Christmas when the ghouls of October had long since passed.

During my time at home, I'd secure Christmas work, then sales and promotions work until the new holiday season began in Greece. It was the perfect arrangement.

When the police stopped calling, my brother Michael – a police officer himself – contacted Nottinghamshire force headquarters to tell them to get in touch with him if there were any new developments. It was vital that I didn't miss anything just because I was living and working in another country. Michael even gave the detectives his unique police badge number so that he could always be traced. But the call never came.

By this time, I had made lots of friends in Greece and I needed to decide what I was going to do. I could either make my home there or return to the UK. In the end, Greece won. I rented a house and bought new furniture to make my life as comfortable as possible. It was an older-style property in a little village called Ambelokipi. It had two bedrooms, a lounge, a kitchen and a bathroom. It was small inside but, when I went to view it, I saw something which changed my mind and made me fall in love with the place. The property boasted its very own beautiful long balcony, which caught the rays of the sun at all times of the day. It also had a very large garden. This needed a bit of work as the grass was yellow, wispy and overgrown. I promised myself I would make a start on it as soon as I was settled in.

A few days after moving in, I awoke and strolled out on to the balcony to take in the morning sun and enjoy a light breakfast. But when I sat down and looked down into my garden I could hardly believe my eyes. My Greek neighbour – a farmer – had put his sheep and goats on my lawn to eat all the grass! It made me chuckle to see a load of farm animals milling about in my new garden. But it solved a problem – I'd wondered how on earth I would tackle it without a strong lawnmower.

Unlike in England, my Greek neighbours were pretty relaxed when it came to property boundaries. It was all part of village life and I made lots of friends.

One day, I was just settling down to a spot of housework on one of my rare days off from work, when I heard a tap at my front door. I opened it to find a wise old Greek lady standing there. She was the matriarch of the village and highly respected. In other words, what she said went.

'Come with me,' she instructed in Greek, waving her crooked hand towards herself to beckon me to follow.

I only half-understood but followed her anyway, not having a clue where she was taking me. The heat from the midday sun was scorching and I wondered how she stayed cool dressed in her long black skirt and shawl and thick black stockings. I also wondered how long we would walk for until, suddenly, she came to an abrupt stop right by an overgrown field. The field was shabby, neglected and full of what I can only describe as weeds.

The old lady went into the field and turned back to face me; I guessed that she wanted me to follow. I was puzzled.

'Horta!' she exclaimed, as she picked a wide green leaf and waved it in front of my face. It looked just like a dandelion leaf. I was baffled. The lady pointed to the other varieties of weeds and gestured as if she were cooking and eating them.

Now I understood. I nodded my head to show her that I did.

The old woman explained in Greek and broken english that if I wanted to be a proper villager then I had to learn how to collect the different leaves and cook this dish from the wild.

'This is what we do,' she told me in Greek.

That day, we collected armfuls of wild leaves before making our way back to her house. Once there, she showed me how to clean, cook and even how to eat it. Once it had been wilted over a hot stove, the horta looked just like spinach. It was served with olive oil and drizzled with lemon juice and tasted surprisingly nice. The lady told me that the locals served it mostly in winter – it was the Greek equivalent to British greens. The tourists never ate it though; she explained this by pinching her nose and turning it up with the tip of one finger.

After the day with the old lady, I returned home a little muddy but full of wisdom from my Greek experience. I found it quite amusing; I was a grown woman yet I had just been trained and schooled like a child.

Later that evening, I called my mum back in England to explain what I'd been up to. I knew that she wouldn't believe it.

'Sorry, Jacqui,' she said, dissolving into a fit of laughter.

'I can just imagine you eating dandelion leaves. How did they taste? Were they delicious?'

'It's not funny,' I scolded her in mock anger. But it was. I giggled too. 'I'll tell you what, though, I won't be going again, that's for sure!'

An elderly English couple lived opposite me and they decided that, as a single woman, I needed to be looked after. They were a kind couple and we became very good friends. I enjoyed their company but it remained on a social level. They didn't know anything about me and I decided to keep it that way. Nobody knew about Colette or her murder. I had decided not to tell anyone, as I knew it would change the way they viewed and treated me. Also, this allowed me to be the old Jacqui, not the grieving mother caught up in the middle of a nightmare. I spent my first Christmas in my little house and invited the old couple to my place. Other friends arrived along with Nikos, a new Greek friend of mine, who insisted on bringing the Christmas turkey.

Nikos arrived with the bird in his hands and a jubilant smile on his face. As he came in, he gave me a hug before handing me the bird I was expected to cook. The only turkeys I'd ever been in close contact with before had been gutted and wrapped in clingfilm from the local butcher. But, as I unwrapped this one, I got the shock of my life. It had been cleaned and gutted, but the poor thing still had its neck on, and it was bobbing around.

'Urgh, I'll have to cut that off!' I said, pointing at the neck dangling limply in my hands.

He looked at me, confused.

'This is going to be a traditional English Christmas turkey so the neck will have to go,' I explained.

'English?' he replied, a little puzzled. 'How can it be an English turkey when it's a Greek bird?'

I tried to explain, but soon tears of laughter were trickling down my face. He certainly had a point, and a funny one at that. I laughed and had a great time. For the first time in years, I could smile genuinely once more. Things were going to be OK, I told myself.

During my working day as a holiday rep, I'd force a happy smile. I'd meet excited British holidaymakers at the airport and take them to their accommodation, dropping each group off one by one. I'd organise the welcome meetings at the hotels and studio apartments and offer advice on local sights and tours that they could enjoy. I loved my job because not only did it give me a whole new sense of purpose, it also allowed me to share in the holidaymakers' happiness even though my own life had been shredded to pieces. It was my escape.

I got on well with my clients, and put myself out for them – nothing was too much trouble. I was making people happy, helping to turn their idea of a dream holiday into a reality. Now I was part of that dream, and I loved seeing all the sun-kissed faces returning home, content and relaxed. My own life had been a nightmare, but being with these people helped free me from it. I was working long hours and, even though I didn't have to, I threw myself completely into my job by going on Greek nights and socialising as much as I could. In a strange way, it made me feel part of a family unit again. I felt needed and wanted by the holiday crowd, just as my children had once needed and wanted me.

Most importantly, for the first time since Colette died, I wasn't looking over my shoulder any more. It felt wonderful. The constant feeling of being watched had disappeared the day the plane first left the rain-soaked tarmac at Gatwick airport. But, whenever I returned home to Nottingham, the same uneasy feeling would appear once more and I'd be frightened and vulnerable again.

Every year, I arrived in Greece in April in time for the season in May. I'd have to be there at least a month before just to prepare the books and holiday boards (adverts for excursions) for the expected crowds. I'd finish in October, but would not return home until after the anniversary of Colette's murder. Being at home during this time was just another stab in my heart – I couldn't bear it. It was too painful and too much of a reminder of everything I'd lost. I would arrive home in the deep winter months. But the more friends I made in Greece, the more I wanted to stay. Soon, I wasn't returning home until January, and in April I would leave for Greece again.

After two years of my half-life in England and Greece, I thought it was time to make a decision.

'This is ridiculous,' I told Mum one day. 'I need to make a permanent base and my heart is pulling me towards Greece.'

'It sounds as if you've already made your decision,' Mum sighed sadly.

I felt guilty leaving Mum behind to grieve in the familiar surroundings of Nottinghamshire, but I had to do it. It was a form of self-protection. For years I'd neglected myself and now it was time to look after Jacqui.

I decided to make a new home in Greece.

It was a happy time and, for the first time in years, I was genuinely content again. I knew that all my new friends – the Greek families in particular – would have no idea of what had happened to me before all this. They wouldn't know my face from the newspapers; they wouldn't cross the street to avoid me. Instead, I was welcomed with open arms and open minds. In Greece, I could be Jacqui Aram or whoever I wanted to be. It didn't matter because no one knew who I was and it was wonderful. Many of the people I met during those early days in Greece remain friends to this day.

When I'd lived in England, I had viewed everyone with suspicion. I would look at all men – especially those with a beard or a moustache – and wonder if they had killed my daughter. It was madness, of course, but then my whole existence at this time had been surreal. Up until the time I'd finally left Nottingham, it was as if my life had been put on hold. I'd always been a people person but Colette's murder had changed all that. Now, at last I was getting some of the old me back again.

In the early days in Greece, I began helping a friend out by working on the reception in her hotel on the other side of the island. Many years later, I was still working at the hotel when something strange happened. I was travelling to work one morning past a tiny Greek church, which jutted out into the road like a sore thumb at the side of a sharp bend. I was just passing the church when suddenly, and from nowhere, I heard Colette's voice.

'Mum, why did you just go and leave me here and never come to see me?' she called.

I gasped and turned to look behind me but there was no one there. But Colette's voice was unmistakable. The words cut through me like a knife.

For a long time, I'd not been to see Colette's grave at the churchyard back in Nottingham. I just couldn't face it. The pain was still too raw. Yet here I was – at another church thousands of miles away from home – with Colette's voice asking me 'why?'.

I didn't have any answers. The experience had left me completely shaken and I was crying uncontrollably by the time I arrived at the hotel. When I walked in, my friend noticed something was wrong and ran over to me.

'Whatever's the matter, Jacqui?' she said, her arms wrapped around me. She assumed I'd been attacked or mugged.

I sat down, took a deep breath and, in between sobs, I told her everything. I told her about Colette, about her murder, about how I'd tried to escape to Greece. Then I told her about the voice I'd just heard from the rickety old Greek church. It was the first time that I'd told my friend about Colette and I could see she was taken aback. Up until that point she didn't even know that I'd had a daughter. But she was sympathetic, listened intently and comforted me throughout. The Greeks are very spiritual.

They believe in the evil eye – they wear it on bracelets or chains around their necks to ward off evil.

Not that I believed Colette was an evil spirit. Maybe the experience was just a random prick of my conscience. Maybe my subconscious felt I was out here having too much fun when I should be sad and grieving. I didn't have any answers. All I know is I heard my daughter's voice as clearly as if she was calling to me from the next room. I have never been able to explain it, even to this day.

Before Greece, I was obsessed with going to see Colette to lay flowers on her grave. The churchyard and Colette's grave had become a second home to me. The flowers had to be the same colour. One week it would be carnations, the next week roses, and so on. If I couldn't get the matching flowers I wanted, I would become quite upset. Mostly I chose white, to symbolise purity.

On one of my visits home, I visited Colette's grave with Mark. We stood at the graveside with our arms around one another and cried. Afterwards, all I could think of was the desperate and utter misery of it all. The grave was a reminder of the hopelessness. That day, I realised how obsessed I'd become before I'd left for my new life. As a result, I couldn't bring myself to return. It would be another ten years before I visited my daughter's grave again, and another five years after that before I went back again.

Sometimes I felt bad – as if I was a bad mother, selfish and uncaring. Whenever I thought of my visit with Mark, all I could see was the two of us, arms wrapped around each other, sobbing our hearts out for

Colette. I knew that I cared, but part of me could no longer visit Colette in her grave without being able to tell her that the police had captured the man who'd taken her life so brutally.

How could I visit and lay flowers in peace without having any kind of justice for her? How could I face her?

I loved my job, particularly the excitement on the faces of families coming through the airport terminals. It was a fulfilling occupation, but sometimes the flights would be delayed and I'd find myself kicking my heels, waiting around like a spare part.

It was on one of these occasions that I met Peter.

Peter owned his own yacht charter company and would wait alongside me to meet and greet his clients. I was struck by his cheerful manner. We'd always exchange pleasantries before going our separate ways. One afternoon, I was standing at the airport waiting around when Peter approached me and we said our hellos. It soon turned out that Peter had something to ask me.

'I was wondering,' he began, nervously shuffling from one foot to the other. 'You don't have to, but I just wondered if you'd like to come sailing with me some-time, perhaps?'

The question hung in the air between us and it took me a moment to realise that Peter was asking me out on a date.

'Er, no, thank you,' I replied immediately. My suspicion of men extended to everyone, even the nice guys. I'd moved on in leaps and bounds in the seven years since

Colette's murder, but I certainly wasn't feeling ready to start dating again.

Peter looked crestfallen.

'It's not you,' I stammered, feeling a pang of guilt. 'It's just I'm not that keen on boats. Besides, my brother's here on holiday at the moment with his wife and they're both staying with me.'

Pete's face lit up. 'Well,' he said, 'perhaps they could come sailing with me?'

'They'd like that,' I smiled. 'But I'm not so sure I'd like to.'

Peter understood, and scrawled down his telephone number so my brother could call him.

I spoke to Michael and told him about the offer. Of course, he was delighted and eager to go, so I called Peter and made arrangements for them to meet up. Peter took Michael and his wife Sue sailing for the day. While they were out at sea, he asked Michael if he thought I'd go on a dinner date with him. Michael agreed on my behalf and readily gave out my home telephone number.

Hours later, I returned home from work to find Michael and Sue back home exhilarated from a day's sailing.

They were bubbling with excitement, eager to tell me about the great day they'd had. I was pleased that Peter had made such a fuss of them. I thought it was a very kind gesture. But, when Michael told me he had given Peter my telephone number and organised a date for me, I was angry.

'I'm not going out for dinner with him!' I exclaimed. 'I'm not interested. I don't want to go out with anyone.'

Michael crossed the room and took my hands in his. 'Jacqui, isn't it about time that you got on with your life?' he said gently. 'Isn't it time that you put everything behind you and started again?'

My face fell into a frown. I didn't know what to say. How could I move on without Colette?

'Anyway,' Michael said, his voice breaking the silence. 'I've told him that you'll go.'

The following day, the phone rang and I agreed to meet up with Peter. I felt I owed it to him and myself to give it a chance. I had spent the last few years viewing every man with suspicion, but Michael was right; it was time for a change.

That evening, Peter and I went for dinner at a local taverna – a small fish tavern in Zakynthos town. He was familiar with the taverna and its owner, as he always went when he was in town with his yacht. It felt weird to be on a date with a man that I knew, but not very well. It also seemed unthinkable to have a good time with Colette dead and her murderer still at large. But I had to do it. I had to carry on living. I knew deep down in my heart of hearts that this is what Colette would have wanted. It was a fun evening, not romantic really, as there were lots of people around. But it was nice and relaxing and I was glad I'd gone along.

A few days later, Peter invited me for a meal at his house. He'd also invited a few of his friends who were all Dutch and very charming. We had a lovely time and my relationship with Peter progressed slowly from there. Later in our relationship, he admitted that, when we used to bump into each other at the airport, 99 per cent of the time he had been there not to meet clients, but in the hope of seeing me. Little did I know it at the time, but Peter had been determined to get a date with me. I was glad that he'd persevered.

It was 1996. By this time I had been in Greece five years and was living in a new upstairs two-bedroom apartment, which had a large sunny lounge, a cheerful kitchen and bathroom. The apartment was situated in the middle of an olive and orange grove. It was my own piece of heaven, to wake in the mornings and to smell the freshness of orange blossom encased in early-morning dew. It was the most magical and unforgettable place.

Six months into our relationship, Peter was talking to me about his two sons and daughter when I began to tell him about Mark. Suddenly, and without warning, I started talking about Colette and the ongoing murder inquiry. Peter sat and listened to every word. I could tell that he was a little shocked but he remained silent until I'd finished. Peter didn't say much, he just listened, which is all I wanted him to do. He didn't offer his opinion or interfere – he knew that this was a personal heartache and there was nothing he could say or do to make it any better. At least now he understood.

We spent most of that summer together. I was due to fly home to the UK in the autumn. I'd already made my mind up that I would go home and get a job back in the UK. I loved Greece and my life out there had lasted for almost ten years. But now I felt it was time to return, as if something was pulling me back.

But when I arrived home, Peter called me. 'When are you coming back to Greece, Jacqui?' he said. 'I miss you. This was a mistake. You shouldn't have gone home. I love you, Jacqui.'

I felt torn. I loved Peter and maybe that love had scared me. It had been years since I'd been close to anyone. Now that I was, I couldn't stop my feelings. Soon, I decided to return to Greece.

In my absence, Peter and a friend of mine had spent weeks decorating my Greek flat with new curtains and new carpets throughout. It was beautiful.

'You've done all this for me?' I asked, tears welling in my eyes, my voice cracking with emotion.

'Yes,' he said.

I was truly moved. It had been so long since anyone had shown me such kindness; Peter's actions somehow restored my faith in human nature.

'Listen,' he said, 'don't stay here tonight because it'll be cold. Why don't you come and stay at my house?'

That night I went to stay. The following day, Peter stopped me as I got up to leave and asked me to stay again. So I did. In the end, I stayed for a week. At the end of that week, Peter had an idea.

'This is ridiculous,' he said. 'We both know what's going to happen so why don't you just give up your flat and move in here with me?'

I looked at him in astonishment. 'Live here with you?'

'Yes,' he said.

It was simple, really. Peter wanted me to live with him, and I felt the same. So I moved in. For the first time in my life since Colette's death, I took a leap of faith. We moved in together in January 1996, and by December of that year – the day after Boxing Day – we were married in Zakynthos town hall. We had a civil ceremony but, at that time, an English priest happened to have come to the Island to take a Christmas carol service. He heard that we were getting married so, on the Friday before our wedding, he did a special blessing for us straight after the carol service. To say thank you, we invited him to our wedding where he carried out a second blessing after the civil ceremony.

As part of the Greek ceremony, the wife doesn't have to take her husband's name but she has to agree that any children born into that marriage will be brought up in his name. When this was mentioned at the ceremony, Peter and I laughed and so did a lot of our friends who were attending. We were both far too old and long in the tooth to be thinking about another family! I thought of Peter's three grown-up children and Mark back home, living with his own children. I could just imagine having to tell Mark and Peter's kids that they were going to have a new brother or sister!

I was happy but deep down I still carried this terrible guilt that I was somehow moving on, leaving Colette behind. How could I feel this happy with my daughter in her grave? What kind of woman was I? How could I ever feel happy again? It was just awful but I couldn't tell anyone. I didn't want to drag anyone else down on such a happy occasion.

Our wedding day was marred by the fact that none of

my family could come. My mum couldn't make it because Ron, my stepfather, had had a series of strokes. My son Mark couldn't come either as he'd recently split from his wife and was now looking after his own family. The only person who could be there was Peter's eldest son. So, as a result, we hardly had any family on the day, only friends. It felt odd that no one from my family was there to celebrate with us. When I thought of Mark, I immediately thought of Colette. Colette should have been there too. My heart, which had been smashed into a thousand pieces, was broken just a little bit more that day.

The guilt that my children weren't there plagued me for the entire day. Not that we were alone – around 100 friends were there to help us celebrate. I was surrounded by joyous, familiar faces, but I still felt so very alone.

There had been no big marriage proposal, no fanfare; Peter and I had just decided that it was something we both wanted to do. I needed and wanted to start a new life with him and, as daft as it sounds, I also wanted to get rid of the name Aram. So much had happened when I'd carried that name, but now I had a new beginning – a new chapter of my life with Peter Kirkby. Looking back, I was trying to distance myself from all the misery and hurt of the past. Not that Colette was ever far from my thoughts.

In Greece, when people used to ask if I had any children, I would tell them I had a son. I'd curse myself afterwards. I'd feel dreadful – the guilt over Colette would wash over me and choke in my throat. It felt as if I was denying my daughter ever existed. But it wasn't that – I acted as I did for my own sanity. If I told the truth, I knew I'd have to explain all about Colette and the murder, and I didn't feel I could do that time and time again. It was just too painful. The bastard who'd killed my daughter had even taken that joy away from me – the very essence of motherhood, being able to brag about your children and celebrate their successes. How could he go on living a lie, after what he'd done, and how could I ever relax knowing that he was out there living his life, while Colette had gone forever?

I was married and happy for the first time in years, but there was one thing that didn't change: I had to find Colette's killer and I wouldn't rest until I had.

CHAPTER 8

THE
CRIMEWATCH
YEARS

I don't know whether it's a record or not, but Colette's murder appeal was broadcast three times on the BBC's *Crimewatch*. I appeared on the show twice. If it is a record, then it's a grim one.

The first appeal was broadcast on BBC One on 7 June 1984, eight months after she was killed. Her case was the first item on the new show and was used as the main appeal that evening. This new style of police show was groundbreaking at the time; British TV had never seen anything like it. All of a sudden, the brutal reality of real murders, rapes and attacks was beamed into British homes for the very first time. Up until then, police shows were limited to the likes of *The Sweeney*, with the dashing John Thaw, or the sleepy, bobby-on-the-beat kinds of shows like *Dixon of Dock Green*.

Crimewatch was based on a highly successful German

TV show called *Aktenzeichen XY … ungelost* (which translates as *File XY … Unsolved*).

Colette's appeal went out to millions of homes, and I lived in hope that *Crimewatch* might help catch my only daughter's killer.

The police received tip-offs – 400 in total – and were able to eliminate countless people from their enquiries as a result. But there were still no vital new clues, nothing to lead detectives to the door of Colette's killer.

Instead, there were timewasters and fantasists with nothing better to do than to waste police time, precious man-hours that could have been spent searching for the murderer. Despite the vast national appeal transmitted into millions of homes across the country, the police were no closer to catching him than they were on the day Colette had been murdered. This situation remained the same for many years.

In 2004 – almost 21 years after Colette's murder and on the 20th anniversary of *Crimewatch* – it was suggested that a new appeal for Colette could be worthwhile. The police officer leading the investigation was a man called Chris Barnfather. He was keen to do a re-appeal, and he called me.

'But I thought that the case had gone cold?' I said, a little surprised.

'The case has never gone cold,' he insisted. He also wanted to know if I would appear on the show.

'If it will help, then yes, I will.'

I had my doubts that it would help, but I had to believe that it would. I had to cling on to that hope – it was all I had now.

So, 21 years after my daughter's murder, Detective Superintendent Barnfather and I travelled to the *Crimewatch* studios in London, to record an interview with Nick Ross, the main presenter.

I'd come back from Greece for this appeal but I would have walked to the ends of the earth if I thought it would help the police catch my daughter's killer.

It sounds ridiculous but I wondered what to wear. I wanted to look as if I meant business but I also didn't want to go on national TV all dolled up to the nines – it was a difficult call. My hair was dark auburn and cropped into a neat bob. In the end, I decided on a bright lime-green linen jacket; I hoped that the vibrant colour would burn into people's memories. It was important for me to create the right impression – I wanted to be taken seriously. I didn't want anyone to judge me or think me frivolous and stupid. This was about Colette and it meant the world to me that I got justice for her. However, I was starting to lose a bit of heart. I didn't tell anyone that at the time, but I felt that, after 21 years, it was never going to happen.

Still, I was nervous and apprehensive. I'd been emotional before the show where I couldn't stop crying, but, as they started to film, I somehow managed to hold it together. A kind of calm enveloped me – I knew that, despite my fears, I had to do this for Colette.

I was taken into make-up and someone had asked if I was OK.

'I'm fine,' I replied, before taking a few deep breaths to control my emotions and keep them in check.

A chill suddenly ran down my spine as I sat in my studio chair and had a few thoughts. What if Colette's killer was sitting at home, possibly with a family of his own, watching me beg for information? What if he was sitting there, hanging on to my every word? What if he knew that, even after 21 years, I was still out there looking for him, hoping that one day the police would get their man? Two decades had passed with him evading capture – he must have felt safe by now, untouchable. At the very least, I hoped that this programme would rattle him a bit, put him on his guard, maybe even make him panic and do something stupid. Maybe a relative, his girlfriend or wife would call in tonight with his name? I had to do this even if there was the slightest chance of an arrest.

Detective Superintendent Barnfather began to talk the viewers through a reconstruction clip of Colette's murder, how she was found naked and strangled in a field. Nick Ross then held the killer's Ripper-style letter up to the camera.

'Do you recognise this?' he asked, pointing at the peculiar computer-style writing on the paper.

Then it was my turn.

Nick Ross turned to me. 'Jacqui Kirkby,' he said, by way of introduction, '21 years, but I don't suppose it's got any easier?'

'No,' I replied, 'it hasn't. It's 21 years but I remember it as if it was yesterday. I go out and I see girls that Colette was at school with and they've got young children. I could be a grandmother by now with the children that

Colette might have had. It's something you never, ever come to terms with.'

I went on to explain how the one person who has really suffered in all this was my son. I talked about how Mark saw Colette in that field, and recalled his awful, unforgettable words – 'Mum, you didn't see the way she was lying there. I did.'

'You never get over it,' I said, trying to find the right words to encompass our loss. 'I'd never wish this on anyone.'

My voice trailed off to a whisper.

The camera panned back to Detective Superintendent Chris Barnfather, who explained how the police had received conflicting reports of the killer's description. But he stressed that they all agreed on one thing – the suspect had dark curly hair. Still, he advised caution when looking at the e-fit of Colette's killer. Also, he explained how police suspected the man had a fetish for stalking girls.

He also revealed for the first time how Colette had been found with a piece of clothing tied around her wrist and that her necklace had been taken, possibly as a trophy by her killer.

Then Nick Ross mentioned the Ripper-style letter again. 'The taunting with the letter,' he said. 'One wonders whether he might ring you tonight?'

'I would invite him to phone me tonight,' the detective added. 'Explain to me why this happened.'

Then Nick turned back towards me and I felt the camera zooming in. 'Jacqui, having lived with this for

21 years, what would you say to somebody who's not sure if it's someone they know but they might have the faintest suspicion?'

I cleared my throat and spoke: 'I would ask them to find it in their hearts to pick up the phone whether they have a slight suspicion or not. Maybe then we might get to know the reasons why and have the satisfaction that he's behind bars and that he's not going to be in a position to do this again.'

The heat of the studio lights burned into my skin. They were as hot as the Greek sunshine, but I hoped that my plea, straight from the heart to mothers, wives and daughters out there, might prick someone's conscience and bring us the justice we so badly wanted.

Afterwards, I felt a bit deflated but, at the same time, I was hopeful. I did more press interviews with the local and regional media in the hope it might bring people forward all these years later. I hated doing the press interviews, but I felt that I had to. If I didn't fight Colette's corner, then who would? I felt frustrated that there wasn't any more I could do. But I knew that I was helping in a small way by doing *Crimewatch*.

The calls inevitably flooded in – between 300 and 400 in total – but there were no new strong leads, nothing strong enough to lead police to her killer. I wondered where he was hiding. How had he kept this to himself for so many years? How had he let this poison fester inside his soul for so long?

When I was asked to reappear on the show four years later – in 2008 – I readily agreed. This appeal would be broadcast in October – the 25th anniversary of Colette's murder. I couldn't explain it but, somehow, I felt the net was beginning to close in on him.

By then, an officer called Detective Superintendent Kevin Flint was in charge of the investigation, and he'd already spoken to me about developments in new DNA testing.

DNA has always existed but it didn't become available to the police as a forensic technique until the 1980s. Everyone's DNA profile is unique, like a fingerprint, but the police were now looking at a new technique called familial DNA, which was in the early stages of development. Kevin explained how it was possible to use this new testing method to link close family members using their DNA profile. It had become available as a police forensic tool towards the end of 2002, but it was still in its infancy back then.

Over the years, the police had retained all the forensic samples connected to Colette's case. A full DNA profile is 20 alleles. Back in 1997, when the case was reviewed, scientists were able to raise a profile of three alleles. But, when they looked at it again from 2004 onwards, they produced a full DNA profile of the offender from the paper towel that had been taken from the Generous Briton pub. It was not only Colette's blood on that towel; her killer's DNA was on it too, linking them together on that single piece of evidence. They'd run this sample through the national DNA database but, so far, they'd not had even the slightest match.

I liked Kevin enormously from the start. It wasn't

that the other officers hadn't played their part – they had all been fantastic over the years – but Kevin was somehow different, and I warmed to him immediately. He was a kind and patient man but he was also painstakingly thorough and always kept in touch. He'd come to meet me if I was over from Greece and always rang me wherever I was just to touch base. I felt he kept me informed throughout. He was wonderful and I trusted him to do his very best for Colette – for us all. If anyone could catch Colette's killer, then I believed that Kevin could.

He'd been a young detective constable – just 25 years old – when the call came in to the incident room on Colette's murder. Initially, detectives had been pulled in from all over the county to work on the case, but Kevin was a local lad and a fantastic copper. As he progressed through his policing career, Colette's case had never gone away. It was always there in the background. Altogether, the murder had been headed by four senior investigating officers. Detective Chief Superintendent Jock McNaught, then the head of CID, led it for the first six months or so, before a lovely man called Detective Superintendent Bob Davey took it over until his retirement. Bob featured on the first *Crimewatch* programme. Then the case was handed to Detective Superintendent Chris Barnfather in the 1990s. Finally, in 2004, Kevin took over. He'd been a young police officer sitting at the back of the room when I'd gone into the police station for a routine briefing all those years before. Since then, his career had come on in leaps and bounds.

Kevin was determined to examine everything again to ensure that nothing had been missed or overlooked. This was good old-fashioned detective work at its very best, coupled with the advancements in new offender profiling using DNA. I put my belief in Kevin. The others had done a fantastic job but, now that technology had progressed so much, I felt as if we might just be able to break new and uncharted ground.

On one occasion, Kevin asked Tony if he had any photographs of Colette that he could have. Tony unfastened his wallet and pulled out a picture of Colette as a toddler. He'd kept that picture in his wallet all those years. Colette had been and always would be close to his heart – his little princess. It was a beautiful photograph.

Kevin was determined to start another appeal on the case and ordered thousands of leaflets to be delivered to 15,000 homes in the surrounding villages in South Nottinghamshire over the next three weeks. It was a huge operation but Kevin was determined.

It was important to him and to everyone else that the perpetrator was finally nailed. Colette's murder was classed as 'category A homicide' – a stranger murder – which thankfully are few and far between. Most murder victims have a connection or link to their killer but the police believed that Colette did not. This man was extremely dangerous and needed to be caught. This type of murder was a rarity not only in Nottinghamshire, but in the whole country. This had been one of the biggest and longest murder hunts in the history of Nottinghamshire police. At the height of the investigation back in 1983, there had been as many as 50 detectives working on the case and, over the years, Nottinghamshire police force had dedicated hundreds of thousands of man-hours to it.

In October 2008, I caught a flight from Greece to Heathrow for the *Crimewatch* recording. I'd been lucky to secure the last seat available that evening. A young man took the seat next to mine, and he smiled at me as he pushed his bag into the holdall locker above our heads. The man was a Greek student who was returning to the UK. Soon we were exchanging pleasantries and he told me a little about himself. I politely nodded in the hope that he wouldn't ask me anything about my trip. Thankfully, he didn't. Soon, the stewardess brought our food along the aisle and placed it on the fold-down shelf in front of me. I didn't eat very much of my meal; I didn't feel hungry, and my stomach was knotted with anxiety about my forthcoming TV appearance. Moments later, our trays were collected and cleared away. I clipped the shelf back up to the seat in front and settled back in my chair.

Suddenly, I felt something warm on the leg of my trousers. I looked down to see that the student had placed his hand on my leg. He had clasped his hairy hand right across it, spanning his fingers across the inside of my thigh.

In horror, I looked from his hand to his face. He registered my surprise but didn't flinch; instead, he gripped me tighter and grinned back at me. I was momentarily frozen. What should I do? His hand began to move rhythmically as he attempted to rub his sweaty palm up the inside of my thigh. I gasped in shock – I was absolutely mortified! Not only was I a married woman, I was old enough to be his mother! With a quick but well-aimed slap, I struck the back of his hand hard and he withdrew it.

'Don't touch me again!' I hissed at him in Greek.

By now I was hot with embarrassment. I turned back towards the window, shut my eyes and pretended to go to sleep. I could feel the man looking at me – his eyes burning into the back of my head. I hoped that my 'sleep' might deter him from trying again. But it didn't. Instead, he began to whisper sweet nothings in my ear in Greek.

'I want you, I want you,' he said, his hot breath catching on the skin of my neck.

My heart began to beat loudly in my chest. I felt trapped and frightened, physically sick. I opened my eyes and glanced down at the metal buzzer situated in the middle of my armrest on my seat. I wanted to press it but I was too embarrassed. Who would believe me, a middle-aged woman? Who would believe that this young Greek man was trying to molest me as I sat on the plane? It would have been his word against mine. Plus, he was Greek and so were the cabin crew; I thought they would be more inclined to believe him.

I thought about getting up and rushing off to the loo to get away, but I was too scared. I was frightened to stand up in case the creep saw his chance and grabbed me more intimately. Instead, I remained seated and watched out for his wandering hands, slapping him any time he took a chance. For the first time in years, I acted typically British.

I didn't want to cause a scene, so I sat there for almost four hours and suffered in silence. I couldn't even ask to be moved either as the flight was full.

As soon as the plane landed, I jumped up like a cat on a hot tin roof. I threw the man a filthy look and got off the plane as fast as I could, quickening my pace as we walked through the airport terminal.

I finally walked through the arrivals gate and sighed with relief when I spotted my brother Michael and sister-in-law Sue. As soon as they saw my face, they knew instinctively that something was wrong.

I began to explain. 'There was this man,' I gasped. 'A young Greek man, he kept...' My voice trailed off as Michael looked at me intently, waiting for me to elaborate. 'He kept touching me,' I whispered, looking either side of me.

Sue put her hand to her mouth and gasped in horror.

Michael's eyes widened; he was mortified. He lifted his arm and placed it protectively around my shoulders. 'What did the stewardesses say?' he asked.

'Nothing, er, I didn't tell anyone. I just sat there.'

Michael shook his head in disbelief.

'I was embarrassed,' I continued. 'I didn't want to cause a scene so I just sat there and kept quiet. Although I did give his hand a couple of good hard slaps!'

'You need to report this,' Michael insisted. 'You need to tell them about this man to stop him from doing it to anyone else.'

I knew he was right, but I was in such a state that I couldn't deal with it then. All I wanted was a hot bath and a comfortable bed. I did eventually report the incident to the airline. Michael was right: if I didn't say anything, this creep would be allowed to get away with that sort of behaviour again and again.

The following day, I left my brother's home and travelled back to Nottingham to stay with Mum. Shortly afterwards, Pauline, our lovely family liaison officer, picked me up in her car and drove us over to Newark station. Once there we met up with Kevin and a senior female detective called Karen. We all caught a train to London so we could do the appeal at the main BBC studios. After we lost Pauline on the tube – she did not get on in time – and then found her again after much giggling, I knew that this day had a really positive feel about it, different to the last time I had been on the show. I dared to hope that we might get results.

The studio was a hive of activity. We sat off-set until we were ready to be called on. Just as before, I was very conscious of what I wore, how I looked and what I said. I had to get this right and nail Colette's killer once and for all.

Once again, I hoped that someone's conscience would be pricked enough to bring them forward this time. I thought that the killer by now must be in his fifties and have a partner or wife who must be suspicious of him. I couldn't believe that someone could carry on as if nothing had happened for all these years, that he'd not raised a single suspicion from anyone.

This time, Kevin and I sat on the *Crimewatch* sofa together to be interviewed by the very glamorous Kirsty

Young, one of the new presenters. They recapped the whole murder case using the old *Crimewatch* reconstruction tape from the BBC vaults, before Kirsty turned to me.

'It's been a quarter of a century now since your daughter was murdered and people always say time heals things. Has time healed?'

I shook my head sadly. 'No,' I replied. 'I don't believe that at all – it's like it happened just yesterday. To be honest, I didn't think 25 years from then that I'd be sitting here. I would have hoped that someone would have come forward by now.'

'Explain to me then how it does feel to have this whole horrible thing unresolved,' Kirsty asked gently.

'There's no closure on it,' I told her. 'People say that life goes on. It does, but it's still there at the back of your mind. There's not a day goes by that I don't think about Colette or what happened.'

Kirsty looked at me and in that brief moment we made a connection as mothers.

'Tell me about your beautiful daughter,' she asked. 'What sort of girl was she?'

I looked back at her. 'She was full of fun,' I began. 'The house was always full of laughter with her and her brother. But, of course, after what happened the house was quiet. It had all gone.'

Kirsty then turned to Kevin, who was sitting by my side. 'The key thing to this is surely that science has come such a long way in 25 years. You were in a very different place then in terms of forensic evidence and pinning things down.'

Kevin nodded and answered, 'We've had a massive boost to the inquiry in that we've been able to develop the DNA profile of the offender – and 25 years on that's been a major boost.'

Kirsty asked Kevin what people should do if they suspected someone – dead or alive – of committing the murder.

'Ring in,' he said simply. 'Give us that information. We've been able to eliminate people, locally, nationally, those that have moved abroad, even people who have passed away because we have this DNA profile.'

Kirsty then mentioned the driver of the stolen red car who'd been seen stalking girls nearby. 'Why can you be so certain that he's the man responsible?' she asked

'Again, through the advancements in DNA science, we've now definitely been able to put Colette in that red Fiesta. We know that the man who went to the pub at Costock – the Generous Briton – is the offender. Most definitely.'

'So,' Kirsty recapped, 'what do you know about the killer? Take us through the certainties.'

'He frequented the Holme Pierrepont area. He was seen jumping into hedgerows throughout the Sunday of Colette's murder before he came across the red Fiesta. He stole that car and then drove it over to Keyworth.'

He then went on to describe the killer who the police believed to be in his fifties or even his sixties. I just hoped that the new appeal might jog someone's memory.

After filming was complete, Pauline and I decided to set off back home. Kevin stayed behind in London with his colleague to help man the phones as the calls came flooding in.

Before I left, Kevin asked one of the studio managers if they could phone for a taxi to take Pauline and me to the train station

'Oh no,' said the woman. 'We'll arrange for one of our chauffeurs to take them.' Minutes later, we were standing outside as a fleet of cars queued up to take various people in different directions. I still half-expected a London cab to arrive and call our names when a big silver Mercedes pulled up in front of us.

I looked at Pauline and grinned. 'This is all right, isn't it?' I said, winking at her as we both got into the back seat.

On the way to the station, Pauline and I laughed as we pretended to wave out of the car window like the Queen.

'No, Pauline, you do it like this,' I said, perfecting a mock-regal wave with my right hand to the city of London dashing by in a rainy blur.

Again, the calls came in following the extra publicity – around 400 in total. Kevin told me that Colette's case had received more calls than any other item featured on *Crimewatch* that evening. He must have sensed the surprise in my voice. I thought that after all these years that people would have simply forgotten about her.

'It's such an emotive case,' Kevin explained.

There had been lots of new leads but still no killer. Despite this, I refused to give up hope – without hope, I had nothing. I had to have hope because I felt I had lost everything else.

Central TV, the regional news channel in Nottingham, covered the new appeal, and I was interviewed by a helpful journalist called Phil Brewster. Another interview was set up with the *Nottingham Evening Post*. I think the police were sure that Colette's killer was still living in the area and we wanted to somehow smoke him out, bring him forward, make him sweat and panic. I thought of all those leaflet drops. Surely, someone's going to come forward with something new? I couldn't explain why, but I felt as if the net was slowly closing in on the killer and that Kevin would be there to catch him at the right moment.

Kevin assured me that the case had lived in the consciousness of the residents of Keyworth and the surrounding villages and never gone away. He explained how some people from those villages had grown up but that Colette's murder was always in the background, hanging over the whole area. Everyone wanted to bring this to a conclusion and get results, not just for the family but for the whole community.

It meant a lot to me to hear that I wasn't alone in this. Other people wanted Colette's killer caught as much as I did. The case might be old but it was and would always remain active until the man responsible had been caught and put behind bars.

I felt more confident and hopeful after the *Crimewatch* programme. Kevin told me he would catch the killer before he retired, and I believed him. I had nothing but the utmost confidence in Kevin.

I hoped this newfound feeling of confidence would

somehow bring things to a conclusion. Maybe – just maybe – something was going to happen after all. I hoped and prayed for all our sakes that it would.

CHAPTER 9

THE BREAKTHROUGH

It was in March 2009 – five months after my *Crimewatch* appearance – and I was at home in Greece one day when my mobile phone rang. I didn't react particularly quickly, presuming that it would just be a friend calling to see how I was.

Then I looked at the incoming number – it was Kevin. He often called me to touch base and keep in touch, so I assumed this was just another one of his calls.

'Hi Kevin,' I answered breezily.

Kevin said hello and we went through the niceties of polite conversation. He asked me where I was. He always asked me this question before telling me his purpose for calling. I suppose it was Kevin's way of making sure that I was in a suitable environment before discussing something as brutal as the ongoing investigation into my daughter's murder. I told him that I was at home. Once he knew that I was in safe surroundings, Kevin began to tell me that there had been developments in Colette's case.

'Jacqui, you know I told you about this familial DNA?' he asked. 'Well, there's someone we're interested in.'

But then he added cautiously that the police were still working on it and so couldn't do anything at that moment.

'But we are expecting some arrests to be made,' he said. 'Obviously, I will keep you posted.'

My heart leapt at his words. I could barely comprehend what Kevin was telling me. *Arrests*? It had been 25 years since my baby girl had been murdered and found dead in that ditch. I steeled myself, clutching one hand against the kitchen worktop to steady myself.

'Wow,' was all I could really muster. 'Really? Well, that's something, isn't it?' I said, lost for words.

'At least it's something positive,' said Kevin. 'As soon as there's anything to tell you, I'll call to let you know.'

I didn't doubt it for a second. Kevin had been a complete gentleman. I had felt involved and informed at every stage since he'd taken over the murder inquiry some five years before. He was also a cautious man; I knew that he wouldn't tell me something if he wasn't absolutely sure of it. I felt a small flicker of hope burn in my heart. Could we really be getting close to capturing the monster that had done this to my lovely Colette?

A lump formed in my throat as we said goodbye. Sheer emotion began to overwhelm me. Could we really be nearing the end after all these years? I felt something wet on my cheek and automatically lifted my hand up to wipe it.

It was a solitary tear. A tear for Colette. A tear of relief, a tear to betray all the pent-up emotion I'd been holding deep inside for all those years.

I stood that way, frozen in the moment, replaying Kevin's words over and over again in my head.

We are expecting some arrests to be made.

Was there more than one person involved? Were they looking at a number of people? The details were too sketchy to form a complete picture, but at least I knew that something was about to happen. The anticipation was like a big warm and welcome hug. *Arrests.* Maybe now, a quarter of a century after her murder, I might be able to get the justice I'd so craved all these years for my lovely Colette.

I looked at a photograph on the side of the cabinet. I walked over and took it in my hands. It was a picture of Colette, happy and smiling. She looked beautiful and I so wanted to be able to pull her from that picture and back into the safety of my arms. I missed my baby girl so very much.

I began to stroke my hand over her face, tracing the outline of her mouth as she stared back at me.

'Colette,' I whispered to her. 'If you can hear me, my darling, I want you to know that we may be getting some good news after all these years. You might finally get some justice.'

My voice cracked with emotion as I continued to speak. 'I just wish with all my heart that we could turn the clock back and you would come walking through the door with that happy smiling face of yours. I love you, sweetheart, I love you so much. I miss you, Colette. Sleep tight, darling.'

Before he said goodbye, Kevin had asked me if I wanted him to telephone Mark and tell him the news?

'No,' I insisted, 'I'd like this to come from me.'

Kevin understood and said that he would call Tony to let him know the latest developments. I wondered how Tony would feel. I tried to picture his face, his sigh of relief as Kevin told him about the possible arrests. He would be delighted, upset, anxious and relieved all at the same time. He would experience the same set of emotions that I had.

I picked up the phone to call Mark and began to tell him about Kevin's call.

I sensed Mark's breath catch as I mentioned the word police. He knew there was something, some update on Colette's murder. He could tell from the tone of my voice. I couldn't contain my emotions any longer; suddenly huge streams of tears began to flow freely down my cheeks. Mark heard my voice; he could hear me sob down the phone, thousands of miles away.

'Mum,' he said, beginning to panic, 'are you all right? What's happened?'

By now, I could barely breathe. Everything had built up inside me and it all came flooding out in that moment. My head was spinning with the enormity of what I was about to tell my son – the first piece of good news we'd had in all the years since he'd found his little sister's body, battered, bruised and dead in a field. I so desperately wanted this latest development to come to some sort of fruition – I couldn't stand another disappointment. I couldn't stand putting my son and Tony through another 25 years of hurt.

'Mum, are you still there?' Mark's voice was urgent and full of concern.

I tried to snap out of it, to tell him my reason for calling. The words I'd carefully prepared inside my head before picking up the phone had vanished. I was struggling for breath between each deep sob. Finally, I composed myself and began to speak. I told him what Kevin had said about arrests.

'Oh my God,' exclaimed Mark. 'I can't believe it, after all this time. It's, well, it's just unbelievable.'

'I know, love,' I agreed. 'I can barely believe it too, but we mustn't get our hopes up too much until we know what's happening. Until then, keep it to yourself, Mark. We don't want anything to go wrong at this stage.'

'I won't, I promise,' he assured me.

Mark was a good lad; I knew that he wouldn't let me down.

'Love you,' I added, bidding him farewell.

'Love you too, Mum.'

The next call was to my mother. She'd lived through every moment of the past 25 years with me. Now it was time to pay her back for all her love and support; now it was time to tell her that the police were just one step away from capturing her granddaughter's killer.

Peter was in town that day. Instead of calling him, I sat there all day and waited for him to return home so that I could tell him the news. As soon as he walked through the door, I leapt up to greet him. I was bursting with excitement.

'Kevin rang me,' I began, and in seconds I had told him everything.

Peter looked at me; he was shocked by the news, but naturally cautious. 'Jacqui,' he warned, 'try not to get your hopes up too much, just in case it comes to nothing.'

But I refused to be negative about this. I knew that Peter was only saying this to protect me. After all, he'd be the one picking up the pieces if things came crashing down again, but I had believed what Kevin had told me. I believed in him. If he was telling me this, I knew that he must be one hundred per cent sure that they had an idea who had murdered my daughter.

Still, I spent the following weeks in a kind of limbo. I thought about what Peter had said; maybe it would be wrong to raise my hopes after all this time. But what if the police were right; what if they'd finally got their man? I hardly dared to think that, finally, our long years of torment could be coming to an end, that there was light at the end of the tunnel, that I might be able to allow Colette to rest in peace. I thought about it constantly – could it really be that we'd find out not only who had committed this wicked act on our innocent girl, but why?

I slipped straight back into the long sleepless nights that I'd endured for many years after Colette's murder. I was consumed with a feeling of uncertainty. I wanted to scream at the not knowing, scream at the waiting around for the one thing that I craved. I also wanted to scream from the rooftops that that they were looking at making possible arrests. But I couldn't. I couldn't tell a soul. I'd been told not to discuss it with anyone in case it leaked out and the media got hold of it before they had a definite arrest. Instead, I operated like a robot. I went through the motions of everyday living, my life on hold. Would there be something definite this time?

A few weeks later, on 7 April 2009, Peter and I were shopping in the nearby town. We had both arranged to meet our friends separately but had decided against taking two cars.

We needed to do some general shopping and call in at the bank before setting off to meet our friends. My friend and I had met for a coffee at a nearby restaurant. We enjoyed a laugh and a joke before, suddenly, I glanced at my watch and realised the time. I was late to meet Peter. I drained the remnants of my cup and bid my friend goodbye with a quick kiss on her cheek.

I set off for Peter's car. It was a muggy day. The sun was shining high in the sky, usual for that time of year in Greece, but there was absolutely no breeze and the intense heat had settled against the earth making it feel much hotter than the forecast. The warm weather had lifted my spirits. I felt happy, joyful even, optimistic about the future. I'd felt like this since Kevin's call a few weeks before.

The jeep was cool inside as Peter pressed the switch and pumped up the air conditioning.

We decided to drop in at our Italian friend Lina's house for coffee on the way back. Lina is a good friend who Peter and I have known for over 16 years. We love our friend and her coffee. Lina is a typical Italian woman, firm and forthright but with a great sense of humour. I smiled to myself as we drove. The scorched Greek fields and olive vineyards whizzed past the car window as we sped by. I knew what was coming. My friend Lina would always start by asking me if I'd like a cup of coffee. Peter would shoot me one of his looks, waiting for my usual response. I'd ask for a weak one and Peter would smile – we always joked about my bad taste in coffee – and Lina would roll her eyes upwards and tut in mock annoyance before joking that fine Italian coffee was wasted on me. Then we would all laugh and joke about how English I am in my safe choice of coffee. I'd always been a Mellow Birds kind of girl.

We'd just pulled up outside Lina's house when my mobile rang. I rummaged in my handbag to find it, and saw Kevin's name flashing up at me.

Peter had parked the car and was just getting up out of the driver's seat.

'Hi, Jacqui,' Kevin began. 'Where are you?'

I was just climbing out of the car as he spoke.

'I'm just coming in, Kevin; we've just been out shopping.'

Peter saw I was deep in conversation so gestured towards the house and disappeared off inside. He probably thought, as I did, that this was just another routine update on the case.

I don't know why, but I walked away from the driveway and over to my friend's balcony. There was something different in the tone of Kevin's voice. This wasn't a routine call. Kevin had something to tell me, I could just sense it.

'You're not driving, are you?' he asked me.

'No,' I replied.

'Well, that's good because I've got something to tell you.'

His words hung in the air for a moment. Then I digested them and realised that there had been a breakthrough in Colette's case.

'Really?' I said, stealing a breath and holding it inside in preparation for what Kevin was about to say.

'Yes,' he replied quietly.

'Is it good news, Kevin?' I asked.

I needed to prepare myself for the bombshell I thought he was about to deliver over the phone. My mind was racing, and my heart sank at the thought that it might not be a bombshell after all. How would I cope with yet another disappointment after all this time?

My heart beat loudly in my chest.

'It's relatively good news,' Kevin replied cautiously.

By now, it was just me and Kevin on that balcony in Greece – it didn't matter that he was thousands of miles away. He was the police officer in whom I had placed the utmost trust. I sat down heavily before Kevin could continue whatever it was that he had to say. I knew that it would have the impact to knock me clean off my feet.

'Jacqui, we've got three men in custody,' he began. 'There are four brothers. One of them died in January, but we've got the surviving brothers here.'

By now my heart was pumping fast and furious; I could feel the adrenalin coursing through my veins as his words sank in.

'It's looking very positive, Jacqui. But one brother died in January.'

'It'll be just our luck to be the one that's already died,' I said. A familiar sinking feeling came over me.

'You just have to think positive at the moment,' Kevin insisted. 'Because it is looking positive. We've got a pretty good idea anyway.'

Hope began to rise once more. He obviously knew more than he was allowed to tell me at this point. All these years and, for the first time, the police had a serious breakthrough. I wanted to get hold of Kevin and give him a great big hug.

All the emotion that I'd been storing up for all these years bubbled up to the surface and erupted like a volcano. Pure emotion came rushing out of me. Pools of tears welled in my eyes and began cascading down my cheeks. Once they started, there was no stopping them. Relief flooded through me and overwhelmed my body; it was no longer my own, it was as though something else had taken it over.

I sobbed and sobbed. A howl came from deep down inside me, fighting its way through to the surface. It was like the howl of a wild animal – one in deep pain – but now, for the first time in 25 years, that pain had been released from its cage deep within my soul. My grief had finally been set free.

Kevin was still on the other end of the phone and I knew he was waiting for me. I tried to compose myself, but I was still shaking in disbelief.

'I can't believe it,' I wept.

I couldn't speak any more, so I said a quick goodbye to Kevin and clicked the phone off. I knew that he'd understand.

I thought of Peter and Lina. After a few moments, I stood up and went through the balcony door. It was obvious to both of them what a state I was in.

'Jacqui, what on earth's the matter?' said Peter.

'I'll tell you in a minute,' I said, still trying to process the information that Kevin had just given me.

'For goodness sake, Jacqui,' Peter said, coming over to give me a hug.

Lina was baffled by my sudden emotional outburst, and the two of them were becoming quite concerned. I don't think anyone, other than my family back in 1983, had seen me like this before.

'Has somebody died?' Lina asked, trying to get some sense from me. 'Has something happened to someone?'

'No,' I replied, shaking my head. I was still in shock and disbelief. 'I can't believe it. This is the closest we've ever been.'

I said it over and over again. 'This is the closest we've ever been.'

Both Peter and Lina looked concerned and baffled; they had no idea what I was talking about. Lina had been a good friend to me and knew all about Colette and her murder. I'd confided in her around 14 years before. We'd had a long and open conversation. She'd held my hand as I recounted the entire nightmare in minute detail – how Mark had found his sister, the crank calls, how the pressure of it had split up my marriage and why I'd ended up living in Greece. She was both kind and sympathetic. She had listened to me when I'd needed a shoulder to cry on. We remained great friends from that day onwards and continue to be so.

Despite how close I was to Peter and Lina, I struggled to relay the information that I'd just been told.

'They've got some brothers in custody,' I finally gasped. 'They've got three in custody. Kevin's just told me.'

I garbled on, still not making much sense. But as I spoke I could see that both Lina and Peter knew exactly what I was telling them: The police had had a breakthrough.

Peter and Lina stood there, looking back at me in shock. Lina clasped her hand to her mouth as she listened.

'This is the closest we've ever been in 25 years,' I said.

I felt excited but the numbness that I had carried inside me for all these years refused to let me get carried away with myself. What if this came to nothing? I had to be careful not to get overconfident. I'd waited all these years for news – anything – or any scrap of information to shed light on who killed my daughter. This was the first piece of positive news I'd had in all that time.

A quarter of a century of my life had passed waiting for this moment and now I didn't know how to feel. I didn't want to get my hopes up too much, but then I didn't want to believe that all this would come to nothing at all.

Peter and Lina waited for me to tell them more.

'That's all I know,' I explained, 'but Kevin says he's going to call me again later.'

The following hours were a blur. As hard as I tried, I couldn't concentrate on anything or anyone. I kept wondering what these three brothers looked like. Would one come forward during the police interviews and admit his guilt? Would it turn out after all to be the brother who had died in January, only a few months before the arrests were made?

These questions led to many others I just couldn't answer. What would I do once I knew who he was? Would I be able to see this man, to look into the face of a monster?

Kevin had sounded sure about one brother in particular. I trusted his judgement completely. I dared to hope that this would turn out to be the long-awaited justice for my beautiful daughter.

A few hours later, my mobile rang. I dashed straight over to it and my heart leapt with excitement when I saw it was Kevin. Again, he asked where I was; I was in the front room of my Greek home.

'Two of the brothers have been very co-operative but the other one just keeps on saying "no comment".'

I held my breath.

'Jacqui?' Kevin said, as if to check I was still there. He knew how important his next few words would be – they would change my life and that of my family. Next thing I knew, he had uttered them:

'Jacqui, we know it's him.'

I began to sob once more, but this time with complete and utter relief. This time, there were no more doubts. The brilliant detective work of Nottinghamshire police and all the forensic scientists involved in Colette's murder inquiry over the years had finally paid off.

They'd got their man.

Kevin began to explain to me all about the familial DNA work that had been used in this case. I wiped away my tears with the back of my hand as he told me in detail the processes the police had gone through to get to this point.

They'd always had the killer's DNA from the paper towel that had been retrieved from the Generous Briton pub. By washing his hands that night, the killer had provided the police with a vital piece of evidence.

Over the years, the forensic science team had been able to develop this DNA until they had achieved a full profile of the killer. It was painstaking work but we had a brilliant scientist called Tim Clayton on our side. Based at a Forensic Science Service in Wetherby, in West Yorkshire, Tim had helped develop the profile until they were able to run it through the national DNA database. Initially, this had drawn a blank. The database held over six million people on it and, each week, thousands more samples and names were added to it. The killer's DNA profile had been put through at the end of 2007, but there was still no match. However, as Kevin had explained, the police were developing their use of another tool – familial DNA. This enabled police to use a full DNA profile to see if there was a strong link to another person's DNA. In other words, if Colette's killer wasn't on the database, then perhaps a family member might be.

This new search technique was absolutely ground-breaking. Part of the theory behind it was that, if someone committed an offence of this nature, there was the strong likelihood that another family member might also commit crimes too. It was a psychological general theory based on social upbringing. But it wasn't a guarantee.

In late 2008, Kevin insisted on a re-run of the DNA profile of the offender and, for the first time in 25 years, there was a connection. At this time, scientists at the Local Government Chemist (LGC) had progressed the work of familial DNA searching by focusing on Y chromosome analysis.

James Walker, a scientist from the LGC, had rung Kevin at work to say that he might have found a potential Y chromosome match between Colette's killer and a young man whose DNA had been added to the database – there was a potential family match. The scientists were able to mark the Y chromosome in the killer's profile and it showed strong potential links to the new profile. Armed with this information, Kevin and his team soon set to work researching this lad's background. Not only did this family come from Nottinghamshire, they also came from South Nottinghamshire.

The police then drafted a family tree. There were four brothers who could be this boy's natural father. One had died and been cremated a few months earlier but the police had obtained a DNA sample from him. He'd been a heart patient at the local hospital and, armed with consent from his family, detectives were able to obtain his DNA and rule him out completely.

Arrests were indeed made, but only one of the three surviving brothers had continued to say 'no comment'– his name was Paul Hutchinson. Hutchinson's brothers were able to recall Colette's murder, but gave concise and accurate statements to the police as to where they'd been at that time. They had been more than helpful in police interviews and had provided everything that had been asked of them; only Paul Hutchinson remained reticent.

Upon their arrests, the police had obtained DNA samples from all the brothers. These were fast-tracked through the system the same day and, at 10pm that evening, Kevin received a call from scientist Tim Clayton at the Forensic Science Service up in Wetherby.

'Mr Flint,' he said, 'we've got a match.'

The two men absorbed the enormity of that confirmation. A quarter of a century of fine police and scientific work had finally brought Colette's killer to book.

'Paul Hutchinson's DNA matches the DNA that we found on the paper towel,' Tim told him.

Kevin and Tim knew then that they'd got their man. But the case had to be watertight. After all this time, they needed to be sure that they got this absolutely right. Thirty minutes later, Kevin's phone rang again. This time, it was someone from the fingerprint bureau. The fingerprint found on the letter exactly matched that of

Paul Hutchinson. Fingerprints, like DNA, are unique to each and every person. This was definite proof that he'd not only killed Colette, but also written the cocky Ripper-style letter taunting detectives as they worked around the clock trying to find him.

I listened in wonderment as Kevin explained everything.

The killer's youngest son had been arrested for a road traffic offence and taken back to the station where he'd been routinely swabbed for his DNA. This had then been entered into the national DNA database. Ultimately, this linked him to his father. Paul Hutchinson had been tested and not only did his DNA match the paper towel, but it was also his fingerprint found on the letter. His two other surviving brothers had now been completely ruled out of the inquiry. Kevin said he knew he had the right man, and that he would be charged and going to court.

'I want to be there,' I told him urgently. 'I want to see him.'

'It might not be worth it, Jacqui,' Kevin said, knowing that this first appearance would be very brief.

'I don't care,' I insisted, rage brewing in my voice. 'I want to see what this bastard looks like. I've lived in fear of this man for 25 years. I need to know.'

But Kevin didn't want me travelling thousands of miles for what would be an appearance of perhaps a couple of minutes. I was told to wait until the next time he was in court so that I could get a good look at the man who killed my daughter.

I was sworn to secrecy. Kevin told me that the arrest hadn't hit the news yet. No one knew other than Mark,

Tony, Mum and me. I'd rung Mark and my mother to tell them, but that was it.

I rang Mark first. The phone rang a few times before he picked it up. He said 'hi' casually, completely unaware of what I was about to tell him. I asked him to sit down as I had something to tell him.

'What?' he asked anxiously.

'They've arrested someone for Colette's murder. A man called Paul Hutchinson.'

There was a pause. I could sense Mark's brain whirring away, trying to place the name. I'd done exactly the same when Kevin had told me.

'I've never heard of him,' he concluded.

It was no one we knew. A complete stranger had killed her. There was a few seconds of silence before Mark spoke again.

'I can't believe it,' he said, his voice awash with relief. 'Really?'

'Really,' I answered, tears welling up in my eyes. 'I'm not joking, Mark – it's true.'

'I can't believe it,' he gasped. 'After all this time, after all these years. I just can't believe it.'

'Neither can I, Mark, neither can I.'

With that I began to sob. Mark was upset – I could hear it in his voice – but he tried to keep his emotions in check. Still, our voices both betrayed relief, vast emotion and grief.

I could tell that this news had brought it all back to Mark. In the space of a few seconds, he was back there at the scene. Back in that field on the morning the police found Colette's naked and battered body. I could tell now that he was visualising the horror that even 25 years had failed to erase from his memory. The moment of finding his sister was burned deep into his memory. It was a hot iron that had branded him internally and left a scar he would carry forever. Now that scar was picked open and bleeding once more.

I needed to leave Mark to deal with these new feelings of relief, delayed anger and disbelief, to come to terms with the idea that we might finally get justice for his little sister. I told him how much I loved him and then replaced the receiver.

Mark had promised not to breathe a word to anyone as the police didn't want it to leak out from the family. I knew that – given how much he had held inside for all these years – this piece of good news would not be hard for him to keep to himself. Now he could sleep at night knowing that the police had caught the man responsible for murdering and battering his little sister. I hoped that in some small way it might help ease his suffering, though I knew that nothing would ever completely heal him of what he'd witnessed on that cold October morning.

I picked up the phone once more, this time to call my mother and tell her the news. Up until that point, I'd been asked not to tell a soul and, besides Mark and my husband, I'd not spoken to anyone about the upcoming court appearance of Colette's killer. Tony had been kept informed separately.

I picked up the phone and dialled my mother thousands

of miles away in Nottingham. I told her the killer was in custody.

I could physically feel my mother reeling back in shock. The news had been like a smack across her face, sudden and unexpected. The pain smarted inside as she absorbed it and tried to make sense of what I was saying.

'Kevin Flint has just rung me to tell me that they've made an arrest. They've got him, Mum – a man called Paul Hutchinson – they've caught him after all this time. They've got the bastard who killed my Colette.'

Mum was silent save for an astonished gasp on the other end of the crackling phone line. The silence hung until, suddenly, she spoke. 'Tell me more, tell me more, Jacqui,' she demanded. 'Who is he?'

'I don't know,' I replied truthfully. 'But what I'm telling you is strictly confidential – you mustn't say anything to anyone, Mum. It's very important this does not leak out.'

Mum promised not to breathe a word to anyone.

'I'm coming over to England,' I said. 'I want to see what this bastard looks like.'

'Come and stay with me,' she offered.

I agreed.

With my plane ticket booked, I could almost taste the moment that I finally got to look my daughter's killer directly in the eye.

Paul Hutchinson. The man that had haunted me in my every waking hour, every day, every year. This was a man who had stolen Colette's life from her just as it was about to begin.

I wanted to come face to face with him. And, before long, I knew I would.

CHAPTER 10

JUSTICE

I felt sick with fear, apprehension and anger as I walked into Nottingham Crown Court and took my place in the public gallery on Monday, 13 July 2009.

This was only going to be a five-minute hearing, the police had warned me. I didn't care – I needed to see him, the monster that had haunted me in my nightmares. Colette's life had been stolen by this evil bastard, but he'd taken her innocence too. He'd taken her from us and now I wanted to be here to watch him squirm and suffer. It had been a cat-and-mouse game for all these years but now he was the frightened rodent fighting for his freedom.

The courtroom was packed with the country's media; journalists had jostled for space on the press bench so they could report on a case that had shaken Nottinghamshire to its core.

I wondered what Colette's killer would look like –

would it be someone I recognised? Could I have served him during my time working in Debenhams? In a few minutes, I would know.

My fingers trembled nervously in my lap as I tried to steady one hand with the other, but it was no use. I tried to hold my nerve. Calm, I thought to myself. Stay calm. I sucked in as much air as my lungs would allow before exhaling slowly. I needed to stay composed. I needed to be here to see him and let him see me. Every year of grief since my daughter's death had been etched deep into my face. The hurt and pain was still raw after a quarter of a century – an open wound for all to see, waiting to be healed.

I needed to be here for Colette.

I heard a noise at the side of the court and craned my neck to get my first good look at him. He was brought in by two prison wardens. He walked in between them and, as he did so, looked up briefly at everyone in the court. I stared directly at him, not taking my eyes off him for a single moment. I wanted him to see me – Colette's mother, looking straight back at him.

The man was overweight and had a sallow complexion. His expression was hangdog and his overweight, bloated face gave away his age. He looked pathetic – a middle-aged man with hanging, flabby jowls, no doubt the result of fine dining and too many glasses of beer or wine. How many nights had he enjoyed with friends and family while my poor baby lay cold and dead in her grave?

He limped slowly into the dock with the aid of a walking stick, as if he was the victim in all this. He was wearing a checked shirt, beige trousers and trainers, which were too young for him. He looked pathetic. I felt angry that I'd been scared of him for all these years – a ridiculous, overweight, bloated lump of lard. He was shaking as he tried to shuffle along with the aid of his walking stick.

I turned to my brother Michael sitting behind me. 'I'd like to put that stick where the bloody sun doesn't shine.'

I could tell that he was acting. I could see straight through it and so could everyone else in court that day. My brother Michael leaned forward to whisper in my ear: 'I reckon he thinks that he's going to get a bloody Oscar for that performance.'

My family and I had all entered court together but we'd been separated by the court ushers. Mark was next to me but Tony was seated at the other side of the aisle. Michael was behind me and my mum was sitting with Pauline, the family liaison officer. Kevin and his colleague Karen were to one side of us.

I looked at all these people surrounding me in the courtroom. It seemed so surreal after all these years. My breath became shallow, as I watched Colette's killer approach the dock. I couldn't swallow because my throat felt as if it had seized up entirely.

As he stood in the dock, he was asked to confirm his name, address and date of birth. But he turned his head, as if he had difficulty hearing. It made me want to be sick. He was quite clearly playing for the sympathy vote.

'Paul Stewart Hutchinson,' he replied, without a hint of remorse in his voice.

211

He leaned against the dock as if to hold himself up. I wanted to kick his legs from underneath him and make him lie on the floor like a dog.

I soon discovered that he was 50 years old. My mind began to whirr with numbers and dates. How old would he have been when he killed Colette? I did a quick calculation – he would have been 25 years old at the time of her murder. He was a grown man even then – nine years older than my teenage daughter and six years older than Mark.

I wondered if my children had passed him before on the street. I knew by looking at him that my lovely Colette wouldn't have given him a second glance, but had he seen her before? My imagination ran wild. Why? Why had he done this to her and my family? Why had he taken her life and ruined ours? Then he stated his current address. He lived nearby – something that I'd always known in my heart.

Still I continued to stare. My eyes burned into his skull. I wanted to be able to look inside his head and see the secrets he knew from that night. I wanted to know why he'd done what he'd done.

Suddenly, he turned his head to face me.

He was staring directly at me. I continued to hold my nerve. Pure hatred flashed through my body like huge shocks of electricity as I found it harder and harder to breathe normally.

He looked smug. A half-smile spread across his doughy face. I wanted to climb over the bench in front of me and rip out the bastard's throat with my bare hands. Instead,

I inhaled another deep breath and allowed the edges of my sharp fingernails to dig and cut into the skin of my clenched palm.

He gave me the creeps. I concentrated hard on his face. Had I seen him before now? I despised the way he kept staring back at me – he was trying to intimidate me. I wanted to jump up and scream at him. My heart was pounding so loudly in my chest that I thought everyone might hear the hatred for this man pumping through my veins.

I wanted to hurt him. Smack him, a clean punch right in the face. I imagined inflicting real pain on him – the sensation and joy of it felt so sweet that I could almost taste it. I wanted to dissect him with my fingernails, sharpen them up, just for the job. But, whatever I did to him, it would in no way make up for the pain that he'd inflicted on my baby.

Paul Hutchinson didn't enter a plea. Instead, he was remanded in custody and another date was set with the court for him to appear again.

He still looked smug and self-satisfied. I soon found out why. Legal papers weren't ready so the hearing was adjourned and he was remanded in custody until 5 October, when he would have to return to crown court to enter a plea. The trial was scheduled to take place starting Monday, 25 January 2010. At least now we had a date.

The judge got up to leave the court, so we were all instructed to stand. Hutchinson himself was led from the court. He shuffled away from the dock, still looking me right in the eye. It took all the strength I had not to leap at him like a wild animal and claw at him until there was nothing left. I wanted to see him suffer, but not yet, not today. I wanted this to be a long and painful process – to make him suffer as we had.

I'd travelled thousands of miles for this moment but it had been worth the journey just to see what the bastard looked like. Nevertheless, I felt pretty hopeless because, despite all the evidence stacked against him, he refused to admit his guilt. I wanted to shake it out of him. I was emotionally drained yet angry.

I glanced at Tony and Mark – we all looked numb, united in grief yet, at the same time, completely isolated because of the trial which now faced us.

Afterwards, I spent just over two weeks in Nottingham before returning home to Greece.

On 5 October 2009 – almost 26 years to the day after he murdered my daughter – Paul Hutchinson entered a plea of not guilty. I felt sick when I heard. How dare he? How dare he not admit what everyone knew – that he'd done this vile thing and taken a young girl's life? I was incandescent with rage.

Before the hearing and, as part of his defence statement, this callous monster had decided to blame his dead brother Gerhard, who had been cremated in January. But, unbeknown to Hutchinson, Gerhard had already been ruled out of the investigation by police using his DNA. It had confirmed, without a doubt, that Gerhard had not been responsible in any way for the murder. Hutchinson's statement only proved to detectives what lengths their suspect would go to to try to exonerate himself; he was prepared to blame his dead brother for a crime he'd not committed, all the time smugly thinking to himself that he was in the clear because poor Gerhard had been cremated.

In court, Hutchinson stared at me as he had done before. I held his eyes and regarded him with a look of pure disgust.

After the hearing, I turned to Kevin and my brother Michael. 'Was it my imagination or was he trying to stare me out?'

They said they had noticed it, and fully agreed with me.

'But how would he know it was me?' I said. 'How would he know I'm Colette's mother?'

I'd forgotten about Hutchinson's job – there's no way he could *not* have known what I looked like. Hutchinson ran his own newspaper-delivery business at the time of his arrest. Also, the chances were he would have seen me on *Crimewatch*.

Hutchinson had children of his own – four in total. I'd wondered how a man who had done something like this had felt able to bring life into the world, knowing that he'd taken one. Still, it was the fact that his son had been arrested that had led detectives to Hutchinson's front door, and that had ultimately brought about his own downfall – that and his boasts in a letter to the police that he'd never be caught. But now he had.

He was like an animal caught in a trap and I had no sympathy for him. I wanted him to burn in hell.

After the hearing, I stayed in Nottingham again for a couple of weeks. Although my heart was now in Greece, I wanted and needed to be here for Colette, but, eventually, I caught a flight back home.

It was a cool day in December when the telephone rang. I picked it up to see Kevin's name flash up on the screen.

'Jacqui,' he said, 'he's changed his plea to guilty.'

The call came quite out of the blue and was totally unexpected. I was astonished – after all these years of cat-and-mouse, the coward that was Paul Hutchinson had finally decided to plead guilty, ultimately admitting to the world what he'd done.

'Right,' I said, as I allowed the news to sink in.

'So you might need to come back,' Kevin warned.

'No problem,' I insisted. 'I must be there.'

'OK,' he replied. 'He's admitted his guilt to his solicitor but they can't do anything formally until he's seen his barrister, which will be next week. So I'll phone you next week. Wait for the phone call and then you'll have to come over because I know how important it is for you to be here.'

'Of course, I want to be there,' I agreed.

I explained to Kevin about my fear that, if Hutchinson kept pleading not guilty, all it would take would be a jury of do-gooders to be fooled by his lies. This man was clearly callous and devious, otherwise how would he have walked the streets for so long? I was terrified that he'd somehow wriggle off the hook, even though I knew that the prosecution case against him was watertight.

I'd also heard that he'd been bragging in prison that he had had killed Colette – he was still using her murder as some sick trophy. It was as if he felt that, by saying it, it would somehow elevate him in criminal circles. That it would make him notorious, someone to be feared, avoided even. That it might keep the other prisoners away from him, keep him safe at night.

But whoever it was that he bragged to saw right through him. They went straight to the governor, who called the police. They contacted Hutchinson's solicitor who then went to see him, and that's when he admitted it. Not only did the police have his DNA and Colette's blood on the towel, as well as his unique fingerprint on the taunting letter, but now they also had this new revelation. Hutchinson had hung himself on his own inflated sense of self-importance and now it was time for him to suffer the consequences.

Once his barrister had been to see him and heard the same confession, the Crown Prosecution Service applied for an earlier court date.

Days later, on Friday, 18 December 2009, Kevin phoned me urgently.

'We're due to appear in court on Monday the 21st,' he said. 'You need to get yourself here for then.'

I worried where I would stay, as my mum was visiting my brother Michael down south, and Mark was away for the weekend. No one was around and I felt like a 'Billy no-mates'. Panic began to rise inside me. But, as usual, Kevin came to my rescue. He offered to put me up in a hotel if need be, but also urged me to call Michael, to let him know about the new court date.

I felt an enormous sense of relief wash over me.

Kevin knew how long I'd waited for this day. I thanked him from the bottom of my heart. After I'd put the phone down to Kevin, I called Michael and things went from there.

It was a close call but I caught a flight to England the very next day. I threw a few essentials into a holdall and jetted off right away. The flight seemed to take longer than usual. Of course, in real time, it hadn't, but now I was operating and living minute to minute and the seconds ticked by so slowly. I wandered around Athens airport as if I was in some kind of dream. I'd been angry that Hutchinson hadn't admitted his guilt in October, but now he had and it was a massive relief.

Now we would finally see justice done.

It felt odd to be on that flight, most of the passengers were coming home, looking forward to celebrating Christmas. I was looking forward to celebrating something of a very different kind.

I stayed at Michael's house that night. On the Sunday, all, of us, including Mum, travelled to Nottingham, ready for the court the Monday morning. Meanwhile, Mark came straight to his grandmother's house. No one wanted to miss this day. We were united in our fight for justice for Colette.

The day came – Monday, 21 December 2009. Two detectives turned up at Mum's front door to accompany us to court. There was me, Mark, my brother Michael and his wife Sue, my mother and my cousin David, who had also attended every court case. When we arrived, I was delighted to see that the Godfreys – Colette's former boyfriend's parents – had made it too. Tony had been taken to court by one of Kevin's colleagues. We all met up in a downstairs room where we had a pre-court meeting with the prosecution barrister.

Some of Colette's old school friends were there and had brought me flowers and cards – I was touched by their kindness. However, my uncle Roy Greensmith couldn't get into the court because he got there late and they'd closed the doors by the time he'd arrived. Roy had been Mayor of Nottingham at one point and was an upstanding member of the community; he wanted to be here to see justice served. But, instead, he was forced to wait outside.

Once we were inside the court, it was a few minutes before a hunched-over Hutchinson was led in. The hearing began. I had always insisted that Colette's killer had lived in the village somewhere and it transpired that I was right. The bastard had lived in our little village of Keyworth at the time of Colette's murder. I knew it. I'd always said that whoever had done this must have known the village – and he did. He'd lived at his then new wife's parents' home in Manor Road, Keyworth – just a mile away from where he dumped the car after killing her. This proved what sort of man he was; he virtually had to pass our house to get to his in Keyworth.

Hutchinson later moved to nearby Gamston with this same wife and they went on to have three children. He already had a child from his first failed marriage.

Only someone who knew that area would have dumped the car keys to the stolen red Fiesta down the unknown alleyway. The police had found them a few days after Colette's murder. The alley is fairly concealed – it leads up from a main road in the village up to a small cul-de-sac. A lot of people were unaware of its existence – my aunt and uncle lived opposite it for two years and knew nothing of it. Hutchinson had dumped the car on a through road, then presumably had cut through the cul-de-sac, dumping the keys as he went down onto the main road and then along it to his own house.

Now it had emerged that he'd lived just streets from us, I thought about all the times I'd been convinced he was watching our house. Maybe I had been right. I thought of the long, silent phone calls – I was convinced it had been him.

At the time, the police had insisted that he was long gone, but nothing could convince me. I'd known in my heart of hearts that he was there, sitting on my doorstep, watching and laughing at us. Now I'd just found out that I had been right all along.

I heard things that day that no mother should have to listen to. Some of the things that he'd done to her I'd never heard before. One of the most distressing things to hear was that Hutchinson had put something inside Colette during his savage sexual assault – either a bottle or a blunt instrument – and that she would have been conscious throughout all of this. This thought haunted me. The police had briefed us that we would hear things that we might not have heard before, but nothing can prepare you for something like that.

I played it over and over in my mind. Had she screamed for me? Had she screamed for Tony?

The prosecution outlined the case against him. Prosecutor Greg Dickson QC told the court that Colette's body had been left arranged in an 'overtly sexual pose' after Hutchinson had strangled her with his bare hands.

The court was told that the abduction and murder was premeditated and sexually motivated. He said that Colette was abducted by force and her screams were heard by local residents.

The prosecution said, 'She was a sexually inexperienced girl and she sustained a blow to the head. However that may have been caused, it would not have been sufficient to render her unconscious and she would have been alive and conscious when she was sexually assaulted in the car. The defendant then strangled Colette with his hands and abandoned her naked body in a field. Her body was arranged in an overtly sexual pose and he was later to write a letter to police in which he taunted them that he had never been detected.'

No one shouted out, in fact there was complete silence, but then his barrister spoke. He asked the judge if how long Hutchinson had already served on remand up until this point could be taken into consideration. He explained that Hutchinson had been in prison 291 days and they wanted to deduct it from any sentence given.

My rage bubbled under the surface until I could contain it no more. I couldn't help myself. I wasn't intending to shout but the words just came spilling out.

'I don't believe that!' I hollered.

I was immediately silenced by a court usher who told me I would have to sit outside the court if I didn't remain quiet. It was hard but I pursed my lips together to stop any further outbursts from escaping.

They continued with the same line about how long Hutchinson had been in prison.

'Big deal,' I uttered sarcastically, as my tears began to flow.

I was told that, if I spoke again, I would be sent outside. I just couldn't help myself. How could this man seriously be asking to deduct a few miserly days off his sentence when he'd put us through all those years of torment.

How did they think this made me feel? His legal team wanted 291 days off his sentence because of what he'd already served. How many days was 26 years worth? How many days had I, Tony, Mark, my mum and the rest of our family already served because of what he'd done? That hadn't been taken into consideration. We'd all served one life sentence. Yet, despite this, his paltry days on remand had to be considered.

The hearing only lasted a total of ten minutes. In that time, Hutchinson only spoke twice – once to confirm his name and the second time to admit his guilt.

When we heard his voice loud and clear plead guilty, my family and I broke down. We hugged each other for support both emotional and physical.

A sentencing date was set for the following month. Hutchinson had accepted the prosecution's case and admitted abduction and murder. A charge of rape was ordered to lie on file.

Mr Justice Sweeney warned Hutchinson that he may now spend the rest of his life in prison.

'I am sure that you already understand that there is only one sentence that can be passed, namely a sentence of life imprisonment,' he said. 'The minimum term you must serve before you can be considered for parole may be that you must serve a whole life sentence.'

The court then adjourned and broke for the Christmas break.

Now we would have to wait until the following year – only a matter of weeks away – for our justice.

Later, the prosecution barrister explained to me that, although Hutchinson had been arrested in 2009, his sentence had to reflect the sentencing of 1983, when he'd committed the crime.

'But he's been caught now,' I said, exasperated.

The barrister was a kind man. He understood my frustration but the law was the law and, if they didn't sentence him as they would have done back when the murder had been committed, then Hutchinson could have grounds to appeal that it hadn't been fair and just. Unbelievable. The rights of the killer seemed to carry more weight than the rights of the victim.

Christmas was hard, but I was determined just to get through it so we could face the New Year with the prospect of Colette's killer being jailed for life. I stayed with Mark, while Michael, Sue and Mum drove back down south for Christmas.

Mark and I were inundated with journalists banging at the door. Then, just before Christmas, a photograph emerged of my uncle Roy Greensmith shaking hands with Colette's killer. Roy had been Mayor of Nottingham at the time the picture was taken. We were mortified. I knew that my uncle Roy would be distraught when he saw the photo. It was another sick and twisted coincidence in this case. I was so distressed that I spoke to Kevin about it.

Meanwhile, my poor uncle was approached in a pub by a stranger who asked him about the photo and why he would be shaking Hutchinson's hand.

'Do you think that if I had known who he was I would have shaken his hand?' he asked, incredulous. 'I would have strangled him. She was my niece, for God's sake!'

It was a horrible and stressful time for all the family.

It was during the Christmas holiday that Mark suggested we go for a drink. I wasn't bothered but I knew that he wanted to and I felt that he deserved it. We went to a local pub in Nuthall, Nottingham, and sat down at a table. There was a large group nearby, and after a few minutes I realised that everyone in that group was staring at us. Mark had his back facing towards them and so he didn't notice but I felt really uncomfortable. Everybody seemed to be looking straight at me.

A friend of Mark's wandered over. He told us that there was a man who'd recognised me from the papers and TV news reports from the past few weeks. It was enough. I broke down in tears and admitted to Mark that I'd seen them looking over.

'Why did you stay if you felt that uncomfortable?' Mark asked, as I dabbed at my eyes with a soggy tissue.

'Because it's your Christmas as well, and you've suffered

just as much if not more than me, your dad or anybody else,' I sobbed. 'You're entitled to a normal Christmas, if possible. I wanted to come here tonight because, if I hadn't, you wouldn't have either.'

'Well,' he said, getting to his feet and passing me my coat, 'we're going now. We'll get a taxi and go home.'

On 25 January, we all returned to Nottingham Crown Court for sentencing. I was glad that Hutchinson had pleaded guilty. If there had been a trial we were all worried, especially Mark, that it would have run over many weeks and into what would have been Colette's 43rd birthday. I'd thought about it too, but now that Hutchinson had admitted his guilt this wouldn't happen. It was a small mercy.

I can't remember why, but in the lead up to this court appearance, someone had mentioned Hutchinson's human rights to me. It made my blood boil.

'His human rights! Where have my daughter's human rights been in all this? She didn't have any, did she?'

The court was packed with journalists and even former detectives who had worked on the murder inquiry. After today, they could sleep easy knowing the man that they'd hunted for all these years would be where he'd always belonged – behind bars.

When Hutchinson was led into Nottingham Crown Court I could barely believe it. He was wearing dark glasses – sunglasses in a courtroom! I'd seen everything now.

I spun my head around looking for an officer to ask. 'Is that allowed?' I said.

I was told it was. Hutchinson was partially sighted; if he needed to wear dark glasses to protect his eyes, then he could.

I was astounded. He'd arrived in court as if he was going out for a day on the beach! However, all that bravado, all that trying to stare me out must have taken its toll. To be honest, I couldn't see which way his eyes were looking now because they were hidden behind darkened glass.

Get used to it, I thought to myself. Get used to hiding behind something because I'll be waiting for you if and when you ever get out. I'll be waiting.

Unlike before, Hutchinson didn't even appear to glance around at anything or anyone in particular. His head was fixed straight ahead the whole time. I wanted to rip the glasses from his bloody face. Unmask him to everyone in court that day. Unmask my daughter's killer.

Instead, I sneered at him as he walked past. I don't know whether he saw me but I felt better for doing it. Glasses or no glasses, there was no more running and no more hiding. This time, he was as good as done. He'd thought that he had been so clever but this stupid man had brought about his own downfall with his bravado. Today, we were all here to witness his spectacular fall from grace.

The court heard how Colette had set off from our home to visit her boyfriend on 30 October 1983. She never arrived. The court listened in horror as the prosecution told how her brother Mark had found her naked and strangled body in the field, just as police had cordoned off the area.

Hutchinson had spent hours in a shed near to a riding school on the day of Colette's murder watching for girls returning home alone. He was stalking them. When he failed to find a suitable target, he stole a car and spent hours driving around looking for a victim. The court heard how this evil man had approached two other girls before he finally abducted Colette at knifepoint.

He dragged her into his car, hit her on the head with a hard object and sexually assaulted her while she was still conscious. Hutchinson then strangled her before leaving her battered and dead by a hedgerow. Her naked body was found the following morning dumped in a field by police, before being stumbled upon by her own brother.

The case – the first ever to be featured on BBC's *Crimewatch* – was only solved after scientists used a new technique called familial profiling. They'd obtained the first match in over a quarter of a century after using his son's DNA to trace him.

Like the Soham killer Ian Huntley, Hutchinson had returned to the village to witness the unfolding police investigation. At the time of the murder, he only lived seven streets away from us.

Weeks later, Hutchinson sent the police an anonymous Ripper-style letter goading them that he'd never be caught. But catch him they did. After 26 years, Hutchinson's unique fingerprint was found above what he'd written. Ironically, those words were 'got me caught'.

We all listened as the prosecution told how Hutchinson's youngest son had been held for a driving offence in June 2008. The DNA taken from him had found a match using the familial techniques now available, and three brothers were initially arrested. Two brothers were immediately discounted but one, Paul Hutchinson, was a perfect match not only to the DNA, but also to the fingerprint on the letter.

The court heard how this father-of-four had initially tried to blame the murder on his dead brother Gerhard, who had been cremated in January, just before Hutchinson's arrest in April. But the police could prove that it wasn't Gerhard's DNA found on the paper towel.

Faced with this, and other overwhelming evidence against him, Hutchinson had come clean. He'd bragged about Colette's murder to inmates while on remand before finally pleading guilty to the crime.

The time Hutchinson had already spent on remand was put forward again – the defence said that Hutchinson didn't want to die in prison.

'Oh poor thing,' I said, speaking out. 'Wouldn't want to die in prison, what about my poor daughter? He left her dying in a hedge bottom.'

I was silenced immediately, and afterwards I held my tongue. I had to be careful – I didn't want anything or anyone to detract from his sentencing.

Impact statements were read from each member of my immediate family – Tony, Mark and me. I knew that my and Tony's statements would be similar in terms of describing our loss, but what I wasn't prepared for was what Mark had written in his.

The court heard that, since her murder, every time Colette's name was mentioned, all Mark would see was her battered body at the bottom of that hedgerow. The impact of that day – of witnessing what this evil man had done to his sister – had voided Mark's mind of all their happy childhood memories. Instead, they had been replaced with one image and one image only – Colette's naked body, beaten senseless by Hutchinson, disposed of like a piece of rubbish, left there with no dignity, not even in death. She was abandoned, dead and exposed for anyone to find. Little did Hutchinson know when he left Colette that one of the first people to stumble upon the scene would be her own brother.

The image had affected Mark more deeply than anyone could ever imagine. But now Mark, like the rest of us, was here and he finally had his day in court. He could see the man who had done that despicable thing to Colette. He was here to see Hutchinson punished for what he'd done.

I glanced around the courtroom. You could have heard a pin drop. Mark's heartbreaking statement had made a huge impact on everyone sitting in court. Surely, no matter how much time Hutchinson had spent on remand, his suffering and loss of freedom wasn't even a drop in the ocean compared to our own pain and grief.

I knotted my hands tightly, entwining my fingers together, making a huge balled fist in my lap. I held my breath as the judge, Mr Justice Flaux, began to sum up. He asked Hutchinson to stand as he told him that he had subjected Colette to 'unimaginable terror and degradation'.

'Less than an hour after killing her,' said Judge Flaux, 'you calmly walked into a local pub and ordered a meal and drink as if nothing had happened, subsequently abandoning the car. Just over a fortnight later, you wrote a letter to the police taunting them and indicating knowledge of the killing.

'Despite the extensive enquiries of the police, the featuring of this case more than once on BBC *Crimewatch*, the killer was never found. Over the years, through developments in forensic science, DNA evidence was obtained and refined, enabling the police first to narrow the suspects down to you and your three brothers and eventually to eliminate your brothers as well on the basis of their full DNA profile.

'...Initially, you denied any involvement, but as recently as 30 October last year, you served a defence statement which implicated your deceased brother, Gerhard, as the killer.'

Turning to Hutchinson, who was standing in the dock, Mr Justice Flaux added, 'It's clear from the defence statement and other material before the court that you are a compulsive liar and fantasist.

'It was not until 21 December of last year, more than 26 years after the murder of Colette Aram, that you finally admitted that you were the murderer and pleaded guilty. During that period, you have lived your life with your wife and children who were, of course, completely ignorant of who you really were.

'But whilst you have lived your life, in a very real sense you deprived Colette's family of their lives, not only through the horror of their daughter and sister having been murdered but through the fact that for all those years they knew that the killer had not been found and could have no comfort and closure in relation to this terrible act. The marriage of her parents was broken apart by all this. The impact on their other child Mark, who saw his sister's body in the field and who is still haunted by it, has clearly been profound.

'The community of Keyworth were all affected by the murder and changed forever by the knowledge that this terrible act had taken place in their village and by suspicion, correct as it transpired, that it had been committed by someone within their community.'

With that, Mr Justice Flaux jailed my daughter's killer for life, with a minimum tariff of 25 years.

This was the moment I'd been waiting for, but, when it finally came, I somehow felt cheated.

It left me feeling slightly hollow inside. Life should mean life, I thought. However, I was later reassured by the Crown Prosecution Service that he would serve 25 years, almost as long as it had taken us to get our day in this court. After that, if he applied for parole, I was told that he wouldn't necessarily get it.

No one made a sound as Hutchinson was led down but I was later told that there was a woman at the back of the court who was crying to herself. I'm still not sure who this lady was. Others heard her weep but I didn't. I'd blocked out all the surrounding noise; all I wanted to do was focus on that bastard as he got his just deserts. Up until then, it was the only time that he'd not tried to stare me out in court – not that he could with sunglasses, but he didn't even turn his head in my direction. As they led him from the dock, I wondered if, finally, the bastard had realised that there was no more running, no more hiding. He'd just been unmasked as the cold-blooded killer he was. Now, after all this time, he would be punished.

No one cheered as he was led off down the stairs to the holding cells below. I craned my neck to get my very last glance at him as he disappeared from view, bobbing down each step with his head hung low.

You might well hang your head in shame, I thought. I hope that you rot in hell.

It was over. After 26 long years, our torment was over.

For the next few minutes, no one from my family made a sound. Instead, we sat in a dignified silence reflecting on Colette and what could have been, what we'd lost as a family. I prayed that my lovely daughter was up there looking down on us all, knowing that, through Kevin and his team and all the countless other officers who had gone before, we had finally got justice for her.

Lots of shocking things came out that day but none more shocking than the lies that Hutchinson told in an attempt to cover his tracks. It appeared that he had spent much of his adult life lying. He was very good at it. He'd hoodwinked everyone, even his family – they were victims in this too, but obviously not as much as my family had been.

This bastard had led a double life but now, slowly, the false existence that he'd created for himself had become as flimsy and shaky as the foundations on which it had been built.

After the court case was at an end, there were dozens of journalists waiting for a comment from my family. I was on familiar ground here; I'd hated doing interviews over the years and now – even though it was over – was no exception. Cameras and microphones jostled for the best position in front of me on the court steps as the waiting reporters descended in their droves. A hush fell as someone asked how I felt now that I finally had justice for my daughter. I cleared my throat of emotion and began to speak.

'I hate him,' I said simply. 'We have spent the past 26 years looking over our shoulders, wondering who murdered our beautiful Colette. We can now spend the rest of our lives remembering the happy times we had with her.'

I looked up at the crowd of cameras and familiar faces that had looked at me from the press bench inside the court room.

'You could see that Hutchinson has no remorse for what he did.'

Suddenly, an anger rose inside me. I'd held it back inside the court but now, here on the court steps, I couldn't contain it any longer.

'I would like to poke his eyes out,' I said. I spat each word out with venom. 'My mum has always said that God doesn't pay his debts in money. Hutchinson is suffering now mentally, but I think a lot of it is put on. I feel angry every time I see him. I want him to suffer. How has he been able to carry on the way he has?' I asked.

A few of the reporters looked at me and shook their heads. They agreed that the extent of Hutchinson's deceit had been unbelievable.

'He has still not said anything, still never said the reason why. I feel cheated by him,' I added.

Suddenly, a lone reporter's voice rose above the others. He asked what I thought of the sentencing.

'At the end of the day, he is going to go to prison but he is still going to get to see his family – he will get visitation rights. Hutchinson took a lot from us. He took a whole lifetime away from us. Our lives have been put on hold until now. He has got on with his life. He took my daughter away from me, yet he has carried on living what would appear a normal life. He destroyed our family.'

Then I thought of Colette – the beautiful, vibrant girl she had been. I didn't want today to be all about that murdering bastard; I wanted it to be about her, my lovely daughter. I looked up and spoke once more.

'Colette was beautiful inside and out,' I began. 'She left my house, perfectly happy – a normal 16-year-old girl. She said, "I will be fine, Mum." But she wasn't. That was it, I never saw her again.'

The shouts and requests from reporters rose once more and I agreed to give a few further interviews on camera. Afterwards, I went back into the court building. I felt exhausted, drained by everything that had happened that day. This was the full stop to 26 years' worth of waiting and now it was at an end. I felt dizzy, almost light-headed as I walked down some steps. Suddenly, my head spun and my legs gave way, buckling beneath me until all that was left was my body falling against thin air. I landed heavily in a crumpled heap at the bottom of the stairs. I was shocked and upset but luckily I escaped unscathed. The only thing bruised that day was my pride. It was a small price to pay.

Hutchinson had become tangled in a web of his own lies – the very foundations of his life had been built on pillars of sand and, now that his secret was out, everything had come crashing down around him, never to be rebuilt. Colette's killer was behind bars. My ordeal was over and our nightmare had come to an end.

CHAPTER 11

THE DOUBLE LIFE OF A KILLER

During sentencing, many things came to light about Hutchinson which proved what an accomplished and convincing liar he'd been over the past 26 years.

Fat, balding and in ill health, this pathetic man had by now turned 51 years old. His picture had been plastered across national newspapers and TV screens for all to see.

After the case was at an end, the police stood outside the court and branded him an 'inveterate liar'. It was those lies and his shocking but smug self-belief that he'd never be caught that led to his ultimate downfall and final disgrace. He'd been unmasked for the liar he was in the most public of ways.

One of the most astonishing things about the case was that it proved what a devious and cold-hearted callous killer this man really was. But he didn't just hoodwink us and the police; he'd conned everyone he met, including his own family.

Hutchinson had lived in Keyworth at the time of Colette's murder but later moved to Gamston – only a few miles from where he had dumped her body. I wondered how this man could have remained so close to where he'd committed such a depraved and wicked act. How did he function on a day-to-day basis with that on his conscience? It was now obvious to me that he had no conscience whatsoever. But how was he able to detach himself from his brutal actions of that night? Was he such a good liar that he'd convinced even himself?

More clues began to emerge from his dark and murky background. The full story of his breathtaking deceit had been told to a packed room at Nottingham Crown Court at sentencing in January.

The judge had labelled him a 'compulsive liar and fantasist', saying, 'You have lived your life with your wife and children who were completely ignorant of who you were.'

It was true. When officers had begun to dig into Hutchinson's background, they uncovered an astonishing web of deceit that had astounded even them. Hutchinson's second wife had been duped by her husband for years, as had his first. He styled himself as a community champion as he raised his own children, and played the role of perfect father with aplomb. The supposedly upstanding member of the community was a member of the Nottingham City Lions Club, raising funds for underprivileged children when, in fact, he was little more than a child killer himself.

The chubby killer had risen through the ranks of the

club to become its president, earning respect and praise from all who knew him. In 1997, he was even pictured giving toys away to underprivileged children at Christmas. He was photographed alongside someone dressed as Father Christmas and the then Nottingham Forest football club goalkeeper. Back then, no one knew who they were sharing the photograph with. They had been frozen in time shoulder to shoulder with a killer. No one had an inkling of Hutchinson's murderous past.

Hutchinson fathered four children in total. He'd first married back in 1978 before splitting with his first wife. They had a child from that marriage but then he met the woman who was to become his second wife.

The police discovered that he was due to marry this woman at the end of 1982, but he knew that he couldn't because he wasn't yet divorced from his first wife. They didn't officially split until November 1982. This is when officers believe Hutchinson began to weave lies about illness. He faked having lung cancer to his family, who had felt sorry for him. He'd fooled everyone.

The police were certain that he invented the cancer as a way of putting off his wedding date and deflecting attention from the fact that he was still married to his first wife. But he soon moved on. He eventually married his second wife Kiaran on New Year's Day 1983, just ten months before he killed my 16-year-old daughter.

At that time, his parents' family home was in West Bridgford, only 500 yards across open fields from where Hutchinson would steal the red Ford Fiesta he used to stalk other girls before he abducted and murdered my daughter.

After her murder in October 1983, Hutchinson paid little thought to Colette lying cold and dead in her grave. He revived his well-oiled cancer lie to cover his tracks and his movements at that time. He asked family and friends for lifts to the hospital. He would ask them to drop him off at the doors of the Queen's Medical Centre in Nottingham. Hutchinson claimed that he had to go there for cancer treatment to halt the spread of the killer disease. His family must have shed a million tears for this seemingly sick and brave man. Meanwhile, just miles away, I was shedding my own tears, trapped in my own living nightmare, still waiting and willing my daughter to walk through our front door. My marriage was crumbling and I felt as if I was losing my mind.

Hutchinson would always insist on his family leaving him at the hospital door, purporting to be 'brave'. They revealed to the police how he'd told them that he wanted to face the treatment alone. Detectives actually suspect that all he was doing at that time was walking inside the hospital, possibly enjoying a cup of coffee to kill time before returning home hours later.

To make his story more convincing and, in an attempt to cover his tracks following Colette's murder, Hutchinson continued the ruse by shaving his head to mimic the effects of undergoing chemotherapy treatment. Anyone who has suffered with cancer or has had to watch a loved one go through such gruelling treatment would feel sickened by this act alone.

Hutchinson soon realised that his cancer lie was a handy one to use to explain various absences or when he had no alibi as to his whereabouts at the time of the murder. In fact, at the time of the killing, he was away from home and his family truly believed that he was having a lung removed as a result of the cancer. He returned and settled down to a relatively normal life with his South African-born second wife, Kiaran.

He fathered three more children. When I found out their names, my blood ran cold. Shockingly – almost unbelievably – he gave one of his daughters the middle name Colette. The police insisted that there was nothing sinister in this as his second wife also had the middle name Colette. They explained it away as family tradition. But I did wonder. You would think that if you had killed a girl called Colette – family tradition or no family tradition – when it came to naming your own daughter, you would go out of your way to avoid that name.

Hutchinson was employed as a railway engineer but later worked with children with special needs. His sheer gall took my breath away – how would the parents of those children feel now knowing that their own precious sons and daughter had been in the care of a killer?

Immediately after Colette's murder, many of the local residents had refused to let their daughters out at night fearing another attack by this monster. But years later, there was Hutchinson, an upstanding member of the community and allowed to work with vulnerable children. He also became a school governor.

In a horrible twist of fate, Hutchinson met my uncle Roy Greensmith on 8 April 1998. Back then, Roy was the Lord Mayor of Nottingham. He met Colette's killer after the Nottingham Lions had donated a Skoda car as a raffle prize to raise money for local charities. Uncle Roy shook hands with his niece's killer 15 years after Hutchinson had left Colette dead and naked in a muddy field that cold October night.

My uncle had been in office three times and had greeted hundreds of people over the years at different events and so he didn't give much thought to the tubby middle-aged man standing before him. Years later, when the local paper discovered the photograph, they interviewed Roy and he expressed his shock that he had shaken the very same hand that had taken Colette's life from her.

I was staying at Mark's house for Christmas when the picture was published. Mark had picked up the paper and showed it to me. I spotted Uncle Roy's face immediately. The picture had been taken a long time ago, but I knew the impact of its very existence and publication would send shockwaves throughout my entire family.

Neither of us could comprehend that the killer had met a member of our family. It made us both nauseous.

Had Hutchinson been aware of Uncle Roy's connection to Colette? It wouldn't have surprised me if he had. It would have all been part of the same sick and twisted game that he'd played out over all these years. He'd remained living nearby after Colette's murder, he'd given his daughter Colette's name; surely this man wouldn't think twice about shaking the hand of one of her relatives?

At that time, Hutchinson must have been convinced that he'd finally got away with murder. He had created a false image of himself in the local community of a loving father and devoted husband. He threw lavish birthday parties for his children, and one neighbour later remarked that this evil man always had the best car in the street. He'd been successful, and was envied by those around him. But all the time he'd been sitting on a dark secret, one that had finally pushed back up to the surface for all to see.

He was the ultimate Jekyll and Hyde character. The cancer lies had covered his tracks for all these years but it was his own flesh and blood that would finally see him caught. When the police arrested him on the morning of 7 April 2009, they found that he had posted a boast on the Friends Reunited website that he held a BSc and an MSc in psychology. But this, like everything else, was a lie. He'd said how he'd gone to university to complete his studies. But, when police searched his home, they discovered a forged certificate.

As the family revealed his brave fight with cancer, the detectives were able to get hold of Hutchinson's GP records. There was no cancer – there never had been. The only thing this vile creature had ever suffered with was diabetes. The effects of the condition had left him partially sighted and in poor health.

I was glad that his health had failed him. Perhaps it was the poison leaking from his very soul, killing him slowly from the inside.

With his medical records, the police were able to tear

his web of lies to shreds. The cancer had been a shroud of deceit he'd hidden behind during the years following Colette's murder. What other lies had this man told to worm his way out of any awkward questions that his family had asked? It was bad enough lying to the police about having cancer but lying to your own wife and children – it beggared belief. What kind of man would put his family through something like that just to save his own neck?

Not content with the lies that he'd already told, Hutchinson then tried to blame Colette's murder on his dead brother Gerhard. Poor Gerhard's widow must have been devastated. Grieving for a husband who had died only months before, only to be told by her brother-in-law that he wasn't the man she thought she'd married. Thankfully, the police were also able to dispel this wicked lie and allow Gerhard's widow to grieve in peace.

It was clear to everyone in court that Hutchinson's deceit knew no bounds. He was cunning and sly, a pathological liar who would go to any lengths to save his own skin when faced with the reality that detectives had finally caught up with him after all these years.

At the time of his arrest, Hutchinson ran his own newspaper distribution service. He would have read the ongoing appeal to catch Colette's killer – him. He must have read numerous appeals as he pushed the papers through the doors of all those unsuspecting households. All the time he knew it was him making front-page news.

Paul Hutchinson's story was horrifying and disgusting.

At least now he had been caught and was finally behind bars where he should have been all those years earlier.

At least now my beautiful daughter could rest in peace.

CHAPTER 12

CLOSURE

Hatred is a very strong word and not one that should be used lightly. But hatred – pure hatred – was the only emotion I now felt at the mention of Paul Hutchinson's name.

Colette's murderer had finally been brought to justice, but nothing anyone could say or do could ever bring her back to us. The one thing I wanted more than anything else in the world could never be achieved – Colette would never be back in my arms.

The stress of the years following her murder – the calls, the fear – had shattered and fractured my perfect family unit. That single man had destroyed all our lives the night he chose to take her from us.

For 26 years, our lives had been virtually put on hold. We were a set of people frozen in time, continually caught up in that horrific moment. Our lives had been paused, as if caught on some sort of warped videotape until justice could finally be done. Meanwhile, Hutchinson had got on with his life. He'd taken my child from me but fathered four of his own. He'd had the pleasure of watching them grow and develop into young adults while Colette's life had been snatched from her.

I felt sorry for Hutchinson's children. Sorry that they were linked by genetics to this monster. Hutchinson had had blood on his hands for 26 years. He'd chosen to take the coward's way out, keep quiet and not admit his guilt to a single soul. His children now had this to bear; they had to live the rest of their lives knowing what their father had done. Through no fault of their own, these four innocent children had become embroiled in the same nightmare that we'd endured for 26 years. It had now become their nightmare too. Hutchinson had not only destroyed my family, he'd destroyed his own too.

But as much as I had sympathy for his children, I could never forget what he'd done to mine. He'd destroyed my family, all of us one by one. I often wondered if Tony and I would still be married if this hadn't happened. I asked myself if Mark's life would have been any different. My poor son had spent his entire adult life being haunted by what he saw that October morning. How different would his life be now if he'd not had to witness his sister's cold, naked body, battered, bruised and violated by a total stranger?

There were so many questions. Would Colette have gone on to have children of her own? I wondered. I was certain that she would have. I'd been robbed of all that.

Instead, I'd had to give my daughter the best funeral I could at the tender age of 16, because I knew that I'd never be able to give her the wedding of her dreams. I knew that I'd never be able to buy her the best wedding dress in the shop or marvel at the love she had for her future husband. Those moments had vanished into a puff of smoke.

I'd never be able to hold Colette's children or kiss them goodnight and read them a bedtime story. I'd never get to see what a fantastic mother my daughter would have made.

I wouldn't be able to celebrate her successes in life or hold her hand and comfort her when that very same life threw disappointments at her. I wouldn't be able to do any of these things because he'd stolen her from us all. That bastard had brutally robbed her of her very innocence; he'd soiled her like the animal he was. If that wasn't enough, he had then taken the most precious thing from her – her life. Nothing could mend this, no court case or jail term would be long enough to make him pay for what he'd stolen from Colette and from us.

I thought about my own life out in Greece – thousands of miles away from Nottingham, from my old home. I'd run away. I'd escaped in body, but not in mind. I could never escape the events of that night. When I went to bed, it haunted my every sleeping hour. There was no respite, no let-up from it. It had always been there lurking in the background. But it wasn't just about me. We'd all lived through this constant nightmare but I could only speak for myself. Mark had his own demons to deal with, Tony too. I could only guess at how much they'd suffered but only they knew the real extent of it. It was a personal loss, a personal nightmare, and one so wrapped up with hurt and pain that it had to be buried deep down inside where no one else could see. But it was always there, eating away at you. It would jump up and bite you. It would pop into your head when you least expected it and would have to be dealt with and then forced back down, only to rise up at another time, on another day. But the grief would always be there, deep inside. No one could ever know or begin to understand what it felt like.

All the time we had suffered this, Hutchinson was living a relatively normal life. I often wonder if he had watched *Crimewatch*, making note of the constant appeals as they unfolded before him while he'd harboured his deep, dark secret.

It made me angry to think of him, self-satisfied that his plan had worked, that he'd never be caught. All those years he'd evaded capture and all those wasted years that I'd spent looking over my shoulder. The crank phone calls – had they been from him? Had he been the one that I'd imagined, hiding in the shadows at night, lurking in the bushes, watching and waiting? Had he been there absorbing every moment of our suffering with a sick and twisted fascination?

Some time after the case had concluded, Ann, one of my closest friends, came to visit me in Greece. Ann had been a good confidante to me over the years, particularly the early days of the investigation when I felt as if I was losing my mind. She'd always been there, a tower of strength propping me up through some of the darkest days in my life. As we began to talk, Colette came up in conversation.

Ann thought for a moment. 'I never told you at the time,' she began, 'but, when I used to come and visit you in Keyworth, I used to park my car right down the street and walk up to your house.'

'Why?' I asked, a little puzzled.

Ann glanced back at me and shook her head sadly as if she had held something inside for years. Whatever it was, I knew that she'd not told me before because she'd wanted to protect me as any good friend would.

'I parked up the street and walked to your house because I always felt really uncomfortable. I can't explain it, it was like I was being watched or something. It was really creepy. I never said anything at the time because I didn't want to worry you.'

Ann was a close friend, but how odd that she had had these very same feelings too. I wondered if Hutchinson used to hide in the bushes around my house. Maybe he hid in the street opposite our old Keyworth home. There was a dead end there. The houses ran out, giving way to an unkempt area full of bushes – the perfect vantage point for someone as devious and twisted as he was.

There was a large garden situated on the corner of the street. It was exactly opposite the end of our driveway. Could he have lain in wait there? Could he have been sitting there, stalking us out, knowing when I was home alone and at my most vulnerable? Was he the one who had tormented me with the breathless messages, slowly sending me mad with grief?

I couldn't prove it, but deep down in my heart of hearts I knew that it had to have been him. He was Colette's killer – he'd wanted to prolong the torture, get his kicks from watching us suffer just that little bit more. And I did suffer. I suffered every day. People I knew, friends and acquaintances, used to say that whenever I smiled my eyes always looked very sad. However happy I appeared to be, however brightly painted on my smile, there was always this sadness in my eyes. It's strange how you can never see this in yourself; even when you think that you are doing a good job of hiding your emotions, you are fooling no one, only yourself.

Hutchinson had been the one who would drive me thousands of miles away to seek solace in the sunshine and laughter of Greece, to leave the most precious thing in my life behind – my daughter.

All those years, laughing at us, all those years never thinking for a moment that his past would ever catch him up. But it did and it had.

I tried to imagine his face that April morning when two detectives knocked at his door. Was he frightened as he peered out of the window to see who was calling at such an early hour? Did he know that the game was finally up? I hoped that he'd been paralysed with fear. It gave me a tiny bit of comfort to think he had suddenly known what it felt like to be trapped in his own home.

Now it was payback time. Now it was his turn.

All those years we'd spent wondering who Colette's

killer had been and now we knew. Paul Hutchinson, a so-called respectable father-of-four, a charity worker – a murderer. Hutchinson was nothing but a pathetic liar. A cold-hearted killer, who was prepared to sink to any depths – no matter how low – to save his own cowardly skin. Even when he was cornered he continued to lie, blaming his own dead brother.

Paul Hutchinson was a despicable man, and now we all knew what he had done. But there was one thing we still did not know.

Hutchinson admitted his guilt but he still refused to answer the one question that we'd waited 26 years to ask: *Why* did he choose to murder Colette? Why did he do this to her? But still, even now, even though he'd been jailed for life and was rotting behind prison bars, he still refused to say. Hutchinson had nothing to lose by telling us. We certainly couldn't think any worse of him than we already did, but he wouldn't even grant us that one shred of human kindness.

He was still taunting us, still holding the trump card; he was still laughing at us.

My brother Michael and his wife Sue were still in Nottingham, so they came with me to visit Colette's grave after the court case. On the way, we stopped off to buy a huge bunch of fresh white lilies. We arrived at the churchyard that cold and bright morning and the first thing I did was clear around her headstone. It had become dirty since my last visit; dead leaves from the previous winter were littered everywhere.

As I tidied up the grave, I felt an enormous sense of relief for the first time since her death. Instead of sorrow, I felt overwhelming love and happiness. Instead of tears there was joy at having my lovely daughter back to myself. Colette was no longer public property – until now her pretty face had been hijacked by the news. Now she was my Colette again, and I had something good to tell her.

Before now, I'd had reservations about visiting Colette's grave. Every time I'd considered it, all I could picture was Mark and I clinging to one another for support and crying together. My other reservation had been guilt. Before this moment, I'd not felt able to visit her grave in peace. But now, for the first time in all these years, I could go in total peace, knowing they'd caught the man who had done this to her. There had been so much pain. It had crippled me for most of my life, but now it had lifted. It had left my body like a spirit, drifting off high up into the air. The weight of its burden had lifted with it. This left a fresh space in my head, my heart and my dreams, which could now be filled with Colette. Gone were the horrible memories associated with her death – these had all vanished that day in court. They'd been locked up in the prison cell with the animal that had created them. They were stowed away, out of sight and out of mind forever. Now, at the graveside of my beautiful daughter, I was left light-headed and dizzy with emotion. For the first time since her passing, I had peace of mind.

As I placed the fresh flowers on Colette's grave, I rested

the palm of my hand on the grass covering the spot where her body lay.

'Colette, my darling, we've got him,' I whispered. 'You can rest in peace now, sweetheart. He can't hurt anyone else now. He's behind bars; he's got his punishment.'

Michael and Sue looked down at me as I knelt at the graveside speaking to Colette. Michael wrapped his arm around Sue's waist protectively as they both listened, nodding their heads in agreement.

'If you're looking down on us today, darling, you will know that we finally got justice for you.'

As I finished speaking, my face broke into a huge and wonderful smile. It felt so good to be able to say that one word – *justice*. It was short and quick to say but it carried infinite depth and meaning. Justice. It had been a long time coming but now it was here and couldn't be taken away from us ever again.

Michael and Sue knelt down beside me. Soon we were all speaking to her; the wintry sun shone high up in the sky that cold sharp morning. The brittle rays of sunshine began to warm the crisp earth beneath us. The sombre atmosphere had lifted and the three of us sat there reminiscing, laughing and remembering Colette for the beautiful girl that she was and would always be in our hearts.

I visited again days later. This time, Mum and Mark came with me. It was 3 February, what would have been Colette's 43rd birthday. We took more flowers to decorate her headstone, to show that she hadn't been forgotten and never would be. I'd also bought some colourful pot plants that would flower long after the fresh flowers had died away. It was important to me for Colette's grave to look pretty, loved and well cared for, just as she had been in life.

'Everything is going to be all right now,' I promised her. 'He's going to serve the rest of his life in prison for what he did to you, Colette. He will be punished. He will be punished for what he did to you. He will never get out of prison, Colette. He'll die in there an old man. I will make sure of it.'

CHAPTER 13

THE STING IN
THE TAIL

Following the end of the court case and knowing that we'd finally achieved justice for Colette, I felt able to return back home to Greece with a sense of peace. However, that peace was soon shattered with the stress caused by the return journey home. I left my mum's home in Nottingham on the morning of 9 February 2010, but didn't arrive in Zakynthos until 11pm on 11 February.

I had left Greece for the UK on 19 December 2009 and, as the sentencing date was set for the 25 January, it hadn't seemed worth making a trip home in between. As a result I'd stayed in England over Christmas and beyond. This meant that my husband Peter and I had spent Christmas, our wedding anniversary and the New Year alone and apart.

By the time the case had concluded and Colette's birthday had passed, we were well into February and I'd been away from home for two and a half months. Peter's birthday fell on 12 February, so I was determined to make it back home for then. I'd felt guilty about the dates I had missed already – the last thing I wanted was to miss another and leave him to celebrate alone.

I booked myself onto a flight leaving Heathrow on the 9th of February. The flight was bound for Athens airport where it connected with another to Zakynthos. The plane was the last flight out of Heathrow that evening. It landed in Athens at 4.30am. The connecting flight to the island left two hours later at 6.30am. It was perfect. Or so I thought.

By this time, my face had not only been plastered across national and local newspapers, I'd also been featured on all the major TV channels and it was getting to the point where I was being recognised in the street. I'd planned to travel by bus down to Heathrow but my mum wouldn't hear of it. She insisted on paying for a taxi so I didn't get hassled by strangers.

The cab took me all the way to Heathrow airport but the usual terminal for flights to Greece had been closed down. As a result, I didn't know which terminal my flight would be leaving from. The taxi driver became impatient – he drove around the airport, making frequent stops to ask staff where we should go. Eventually, he was advised to drop me off at terminal four and not terminal two. By now, he was getting a bit miffed and I was beginning to get a bit frantic as time was ticking by to my flight. I needn't have worried – to my horror I was soon reading the last words I wanted to read: Athens flight cancelled.

I was frantic. I'd been so excited about going home and now I was stuck on my own in London with nothing on me. I needed to make that flight to connect with my second flight in a bid to make it home in time for my husband's birthday.

I dashed back over to the handling agent. She informed me that they were putting on extra flights. I felt relieved but when she handed me my new ticket I realised exactly what she meant – they were putting people onto flights leaving on other days. The ticket I'd been handed was for Thursday, two days later. Then I looked at the details for my onward flight. That was for the following day – Friday – Peter's birthday!

I complained of course, but there was nothing they could do. A strike in Greece had caused this mess. I was panic-stricken. I'd been through so much and now I faced three days of hanging around airports in an attempt to get home. We were all stranded. Arguments ensued as people began to lose their temper with the poor members of staff. For me, the whole situation had become too much. The pent-up emotion of the past few months just came spilling out. I pulled out my mobile phone and called my mum back in Nottingham. I began to sob down the phone to her and once I started, I found that I couldn't stop.

Soon the crowd stopped talking, a hush fell and people began to turn to look at me. I knew that I was making a complete fool of myself but I couldn't help it. I'd been through the murder, the capture, the court case and now this. The cancelled flight was the straw that broke the camel's back.

A member of staff noticed my distress and came rushing over.

'I know it can be a very stressful time when things don't go according to plan,' she soothed.

I looked up at her, I knew that she was only trying to be kind, but sympathy was the last thing I needed. I just wanted to be on my flight home.

'You have no idea,' I began, 'I have just been to hell and back over the last few months. My daughter has been murdered and I've just had to deal with the court case. Now I just want to go home.'

The woman looked at me and reeled back in horror; I could tell that she was visibly shocked. The gasps of those standing nearby were audible. My voice softened. ' I know it's not your fault,' I wept, 'but someone should have at least phoned me to let me know. You have contact numbers for me. If I had been told then I wouldn't have travelled all the way down here today – you were clearly aware of the situation hours before.'

The woman dropped her official stance of not being able to help and agreed to put all the stranded passengers up in a hotel bed for the night. As a goodwill gesture, the airline also agreed to pay for an evening meal with breakfast the following morning. It wasn't perfect but at least it solved my immediate problem of where I was going to sleep that night.

The other passengers, having witnessed my personal meltdown, took pity on me and took me under their wing. We all boarded the airport coach together to travel to the hotel and shared dinner together that night. When

I awoke the following morning, I had a raging earache. I knew instantly that I needed antibiotics. I'd suffered with recurrent infections of my middle ear over the years since Colette's murder. My doctor had told me it had been brought on by stressful situations and now, just as I should have felt inner peace for the first time in 26 years, I was faced with even more stress. My body was in meltdown once more.

After breakfast, I asked reception for directions and walked to a nearby chemist to try and get medication for it. The female pharmacist was kind but there was nothing she could sell me over the counter to cure it. I needed a prescription, so she directed me to a doctor's surgery further along the road.

Thankfully, I was able to make an emergency appointment and saw a doctor who prescribed me with some antibiotic drops.

I left the hotel at 4.30am on the morning of the flight to Athens. As it was due to land at 1.30pm, and I would be faced with a day and night waiting for my connecting flight, Peter told me to catch the last bus from Athens for Zakynthos, which left three hours later at 4.30pm. In order to do this, I had to get across the city of Athens, which takes over an hour by bus. I didn't want anything else to go wrong so I decided to catch a taxi instead but when I arrived, I discovered that the taxis were on strike that day! It was a series of strikes throughout Greece and there was general mayhem.

To say that I was stressed out was an understatement.

Once I was home, what had been said in court ran over

and over in my head. I couldn't help it. All I could think about was the horrible disgusting things that animal had done to my lovely daughter. On reflection, I should have taken a short holiday away from everything. I'd gone through a very emotional time and I needed to give myself to recover – to withdraw from the world for a while, take time out to make sense of it all. Back in the safety of my Greek hilltop home, I hid myself away and shed tears in secret. Again I wondered if my baby had screamed out for me. Had she called for her dad? What hell had she been through? What pain had she endured? Had that bastard laughed as he clamped his hands around her throat, squeezing the very life from her? Had he laughed at us for all those years? I had visions of Colette screaming, kicking and fighting to escape. I wished I could turn the clock back so that everything would be OK again.

Colette was so real in my dreams and nightmares that I felt as if I could reach out and touch her and pull her back to me. It was only the following morning that I'd wake up in a cold sweat and realise she wasn't OK, that she was gone and that all those visions and nightmares had been real.

Soon February gave way to March and, before I knew it, the summer season was upon us once more. Greece was now inundated with happy holidaymakers, families having fun. It was always a difficult time of year for me.

It wasn't until the end of April 2010 that I began to feel more like myself again. Mark had planned to come out to see me on holiday. I was looking forward to it, as he would be there for my birthday. On the day, we went out for a lovely birthday meal, just the two of us, as Peter was away for a couple of weeks on one of his sailing breaks. For the first time in years, Mark and I laughed and joked almost like old times. We both seemed much happier, lighter in spirit as if a lifetime of tension had lifted almost overnight.

We spent a couple of weeks just enjoying each other's company. The rest of the summer flew by with the usual comings and goings of visitors to our house. It kept me busy. I visited old friends who knew about Colette and what we'd been through. Most had watched the news in Greece on the satellite TV channels. Many of my Greek friends had asked after me; they all wanted to know if I was coping. And I was, just about.

A close friend asked me to help out with her business, which dealt with internet car bookings for holiday-makers. I agreed. Most of the summer, I was stationed at the airport handing over cars and taking cash to the office. Everyone seemed to have a job for me to do. It kept me on my feet and made sure my mind was active. In short, it stopped me thinking too much about things.

All was as well as could be expected. But, on 10 October 2010, my life changed again in an instant.

It was a Sunday and Peter and I had been invited over to a friend's barbeque. They owned a hotel on the island but it had closed up for the winter and they'd asked us to go along that day for something to eat. Peter's son was over on holiday so he came with us.

My friend's husband had been fishing earlier that

morning. He cooked us some lovely fresh fish and squid on the barbeque, while his wife had made various salads, Greek dips and homemade desserts. We were just starting to eat some of the delicious food that they had prepared when my mobile phone rang. I put my glass of wine down on the table and rummaged through my bag looking for it. I noticed the time on my watch. It was 12.30pm in Greece, so it was still early in the UK. As I pulled the phone from my handbag, I saw Kevin's name flash up on the screen. I'd not spoken to him since leaving England after the court case, nine months earlier, so I wondered why he would be ringing me now, especially so early on a Sunday morning. It had to be important.

Kevin's voice sounded serious and urgent. 'Jacqui, it's Kevin,' he began. 'Where are you?'

I stifled a smile. He always asked me the same question every time he rang, bless him. I told him I was safe at a barbecue.

I knew from the sound of Kevin's voice that this wasn't good news. I thought of Hutchinson – he was safely behind bars so it couldn't be anything to do with him. Then my mind flashed to my family back home in the UK. Were they all right? Panic set in.

'What is it, Kevin?' I asked urgently, but part of me did not want to know the answer.

My friends were laughing, chatting and drinking wine in the background. This was a happy day but I knew that Kevin was about to tell me something that would turn my world upside down all over again.

'Hutchinson was found dead in his cell this morning,' Kevin told me, his voice serious and sombre.

'What!' I exclaimed.

My friends heard my startled reaction and looked over. But I was in too much shock to explain what I'd just been told.

'Jacqui, he was found dead in his cell this morning,' Kevin repeated.

'*How*?' I asked. I was shaking with anger. After all these years, we'd got the bastard only for him to die in a prison cell less than nine months into his life sentence.

'At this point in time, we don't know how he died or whether it was natural causes.'

'I can't believe it,' I gasped. I couldn't.

Soon shock gave way to hot angry tears. They began to cascade down my face until my linen trousers were marked with dark pools of water. My tears stained the fabric on my thighs and turned it a deeper shade in the hot midday sun.

I'd wished Hutchinson dead many times over the years, but now that he was I had mixed emotions. I felt cheated. I wanted him to serve more than just a few measly months of his life sentence.

There was a pause in the conversation between Kevin and me. Neither of us knew what to say. We were both devastated that, after all these years of looking for him, we'd caught Hutchinson only for him to slip through the net of life. I'd wanted him to suffer, but now he was gone and he couldn't suffer any more. I felt a loss, but not the loss I'd experienced after Colette. This was a different kind of loss – bitterness at his escape from life and punishment. Hutchinson needed to be punished but, in my eyes, he'd escaped that punishment, just as he'd evaded capture.

'It's bittersweet, isn't it?' Kevin remarked, finally breaking the silence.

'Yes,' I replied, my voice rendered paper-thin with emotion.

'They don't know at this time how he died. The prison wardens went into his cell this morning to wake him up but they couldn't wake him. They called the paramedics...'

'I can't believe it,' I said, interrupting Kevin. 'All these years we've waited for it and now he's not even going to get to serve his sentence – not even half of it.'

Hutchinson died in prison but not as I'd promised Colette. He'd not died an old man – he'd died in the mid-term of his life. But while she was lying cold in her grave, Hutchinson had lived his life. I felt bereft for Colette, bereft for my family and for myself. It was as though somehow, by his death, we had let her down. We'd unmasked her killer only for him to slip away again.

Kevin warned me that the media would start calling and, sure enough, as soon as they heard the news, my phone started ringing off the hook. The local paper telephoned to ask if I'd heard the news. A female journalist waited for my response to the rumour that Hutchinson had possibly stockpiled his own medication.

'How do you feel about the fact that he could have taken his own life?' she asked gently.

'I hope he rots in hell,' I replied. 'If he did kill himself, I think it's a coward's way out, but, then, he's been a coward from the beginning. I just hope that he inflicted enough injuries on himself or took enough medication to die in a way that was as terrible as Colette's death.'

It had been another kick in the teeth for us all.

Two separate investigations were launched – one by the police and another by the Prison and Probations Ombudsman.

On 24 October 2011 – over a year later, and almost 28 years after he'd murdered my lovely daughter – an inquest was held into the death of Paul Hutchinson. I remained in Greece, but my brother Michael travelled up to Nottingham for it.

The inquest heard how Hutchinson had taken a fatal cocktail of prescription drugs and was discovered unconscious in his cell. A prison officer had found him at 8.30am on the morning of 10 October 2010. When staff failed to rouse him, paramedics were called and attempted to resuscitate him for between 20 and 30 minutes. Hutchinson was taken by ambulance to the Queen's Medical Centre in Nottingham, where he was pronounced dead at 9.55am.

It was revealed that Hutchinson had tried to stash pills in his cell on an earlier occasion. More than 40 anti-depressant pills were found in a sock.

His daughter from his second marriage told Nottingham Coroner's Court how her father had seemed despondent in the days leading up to his death. His wife had asked for a divorce and the divorce decree was due just nine days later. Hutchinson had been on suicide watch and monitoring for self-harm on at least two or three occasions before, but he was not on those at the time of his death.

The inquest heard how he'd died of an overdose after consuming a large quantity of drugs, including antidepressants, an anti-epilepsy drug and paracetamol. At the end of the two-day hearing, a jury returned a verdict of suicide.

Like Harold Shipman before him, Hutchinson had taken the easy way out. Thanks to the brilliant work of the police, we'd had our day in court and Hutchinson had been revealed for the evil man he truly was. We'd finally got justice for Colette, only for that very same justice to be snatched away from her in a heartbeat.

But her killer's death had been resolved in a way that Colette's never could be. He'd taken the coward's way out because he didn't have the courage to serve his life term in prison. At least his family got to know it was suicide and found out what happened. I'm never going to be able to get that for Colette. We never got real closure because we never got answers and now we never will.

To be honest, I don't care how that bastard died; it won't bring my lovely Colette back. The only thing that keeps me going is the fact that he can't ever do this to anyone else's daughter. He can't hurt, lie or cheat any more. Now he's in hell – a place he's always belonged.

AFTERWORD
NOVEMBER 2011

As I sit here writing this, I think of Colette in happier times. Life for me moves forward now and, instead of living in the past, I feel as though, for the first time in my life, I can now actually look towards the future. I'm a different person to the Jacqui I was for those 26 long years. I am calmer, I feel less stressed, and I am generally more at peace with life and all that it throws at me.

My life isn't perfect, no one's is, but I know how lucky I am to be living on such a beautiful Greek Island. Each morning as I wake, I can look out at fantastic views from our mountaintop home – the olive grove and the breath-taking views of the ocean. It brings me a kind of inner calm. It is something that no amount of money can buy and, like my beautiful Colette, it is priceless.

I may not have Colette in my arms but she's in my heart every second of every day. I also have Mark and my beautiful grandsons, so, in many ways, I feel blessed. I am also very lucky to have such wonderful family and friends. All these things add up to a happier and more content life.

Today, I try to concentrate on the happier times that we shared as a family – the fun and laughter of all those family holidays and the fact that as a mother I was blessed with two beautiful children. They were brought up in a family of love. They always knew how much they were loved – a day didn't pass by without Tony and me telling them this. I think back to all those happy Christmas Days that we shared together, when the four of us would snuggle up in our bed and open our presents together. I will never forget my delight and pride watching both Mark and Colette grow up and become fine young adults. It still makes me very proud to think of them both.

When I think of Colette particularly, I think of all the funny little things she would say. I remember her voice; I remember her giggling and laughing constantly with her good friends. Many of these girls have remained loyal to her to this day. As I look around at all her dancing medals and certificates, her teenage jewellery and her small fluffy toys, I recall happy times. Above all, I remember that, despite everything else, we were blessed with a very happy, special daughter.

Colette, you will always be with me, no matter where I am. I love you, Colette – we all do and always will.

All my love,

Mum
x